LIFE IN HIS PRESENCE

The Secret to Unlocking Sustained Blessing

A Guide for Every Christian
Revealing How to Consistently
Bring Heaven into Earth

By

Michael L. Ruegamer

FREEDOM HOUSE
"Freedom Reigns in this Place"

For more products please see our website www.freedomhouseac.com.

TABLE OF CONTENTS

Introduction..6

Chapter 1: The Ultimate Partnership............................9

Chapter 2: Crowned with Glory and Honor..................22

Chapter 3: The Transfer of Authority..........................30

Chapter 4: The Beginning of Restoration.....................41

Chapter 5: The Kingdom is at Hand............................48

Chapter 6: The Father's Sovereign Government............55

Chapter 7: Activating the Kingdom.............................65

Chapter 8: Releasing the Kingdom..............................72

Chapter 9: Naturally Supernatural.............................111

Chapter 10: We Are a Living Sacrifice........................133

About the Author...143

Introduction

I was raised in a Charismatic Catholic church in a small town in Southwestern Montana; although at the time I didn't know it was Charismatic. I remember learning about the sacraments, qualifying for my first communion at nine years of age and being baptized on Easter. I would often pray to God and talk to God but really hadn't come to know Him until later in life.

After graduating from college I was a successful petroleum engineer living what many would consider the American dream in Southwestern Wyoming. I had a great job with great benefits but I always seemed to have a thought in the back of mind that there was more to life than what I was experiencing.

I was knowledgeable of the bible and would attend church occasionally but God certainly wasn't the focus of my life. Even with all my success there seemed to be something missing so I did what knew to do at the time; search for answers.

I began my search in the self-help section of the local book store and purchased a few books that I thought would help. As I read the pages of those books I didn't really find what I was looking for. I was already doing most of what the books recommended.

One day I was cleaning out my closet and found a New Testament with Psalms and Proverbs that I had been given from Campus Crusade for Christ when I was in college. When I began to read the gospels something started happening to me that is really hard to explain.

One day the most amazing thing happened. While I was reading 1 Corinthians 13:13 it was as if I heard an audible voice say to me, "I am the father that loves you and my love never fails". I began to realize that what I was missing and longing for was authentic love that only God could provide.

Immediately I felt an overwhelming warm feeling inside. There were times in my life when I felt a similar feeling of safety, acceptance and fulfillment but never with such intensity. It seemed to originate from my inner core and just overshadowed and overwhelmed me. Looking back at the experience now I am truly amazed at God's desire to meet us at our point of need.

I didn't know that I could cry out to God. I also didn't know He was calling out to me drawing me to Him. I just knew I was unfulfilled and all that I was trying to fill my void wasn't working. I didn't realize my heavenly Father was ready to provide the miracle I needed. I was being invited to experience the greatest miracle of all; the unfailing love of God.

A couple of months later I found myself at the altar of a local church rededicating my life to Jesus and being filled with the Holy Spirit. Shortly after my experience with the Holy Spirit in 2003 I began to see the scriptures in an entirely new way. What was once an intellectual exercise became a journey that took me places beyond my imagination.

I love to study the word. Over the years I have spent many hours studying many different subjects that seem to be the focus of this Christian life. Only one has enabled me to experience the benefits of them all; learning to live in His presence.

According to literary scholars an introduction reveals the purpose and goals of a body of literature. I would now like to employ this simple definition by quoting the words the apostle Paul spoke to the church in Rome;

> *For I long to see you, that I may impart unto you some spiritual gift, to the end ye may be established.* (Romans 1:11)

I may not have the opportunity to see many of you reading this book in the natural but my desire is the same; to impart to you the ability to live a life filled with the presence of God so that you are established in Him to experience all of His fullness. As you read the following pages, I pray that the presence of God invades every part of you and every purpose He has for you is awakened in Jesus name.

Chapter 1

The Ultimate Partnership

As I read the pages of the bible from Genesis to Revelation I see a very common theme illustrated. Many say that we were created to worship. Others say our purpose is to serve. Though I do believe these statements have merit they don't fully reveal the Fathers one true desire.

The God of the universe desires to partner with us to enable us to take on His image and unlock His purposes in the earth. I believe this was His ultimate goal when He created man in His image and placed him in the midst of the garden.

When I read scriptures like John 5:30, I see this ultimate partnership beautifully displayed in the life of Jesus as He walked the earth revealing the heart of the Father. *"I can do nothing on My own initiative. As I hear, I judge; and My judgment is just, because I do not seek My own will, but the will of Him who sent Me"*. Jesus did this so masterfully and then said we could do the same and more. *Verily, verily, I say unto you, He that believeth on me, the works that I do shall he do also; and greater works than these shall he do; because I go unto my Father* (John 14:12 KJV).

Jesus's words are so amazing. We can do the same works He did. Seeing that it is possible to live a life so connected to our creator that it totally defines our entire existence is quite perplexing for me. In essence, we can live a life camped around His presence producing the fruit of this ultimate partnership between us and our heavenly Father. Before I get too much deeper into the scriptural basis of living life in His presence I feel it is important to give my testimony of how God brought me to this understanding.

My Story

Early in my conversion I found myself praying for people and telling them about Jesus with great boldness. I had a fiery passion burning on the inside of me and I felt I needed to share it with everyone. To my surprise most people didn't want to hear what I had to say. I quickly became the weird religious guy people would avoid but the fire burning on the inside of me continued to increase.

I once stood on a small airplane that was flying from Colorado to Montana and gave an invitation to the passengers to believe in Jesus. I told them we had no guarantee the plane would land safely and there was a possibility we would meet our creator. The flight attendant quickly instructed me to sit down and be quite or she would have to remove me from the flight so I did without a single response from those on the plane.

That same day I prayed for a young man with a cast on his arm and nothing happened. A week later I was in Denver, CO at a job related training school. After the school was over I started walking around downtown Denver looking for people to pray for. That night I prayed for many people and purchased many dinners for individuals who were homeless but didn't see any miracles.

I prayed for one man who had broken his foot but couldn't go to a hospital. He had a plastic garbage bag wrapped around it with an old T-shirt and was walking around with some makeshift crutches. I was sure that when I prayed for him he would be healed but he wasn't. All of this was very confusing to me because the bible is very clear about the signs that should follow us.

I went to my Pastor to see why miracles weren't happening. The answer I got was very discouraging to me. I was told that if I brought these people into the church they would be healed and that it was unwise to pray for people on the street or at my job. Even though I didn't really understand or agree with the counsel I received I went along with it anyway. I stopped praying for people in public places and would invite people to church rather than tell them about Jesus.

Needless to say I got the same results as before. Those whom I invited to church declined so I stopped completely. I decided that I would just love God, go to church and work. In 2005 the associate Pastors of the church I was attending decided to move to Texas to start a ministry. I felt strongly connected to them and was ready for a change so I started looking for jobs in Houston. We moved in January and I finally was working again by mid-March.

We were attending a large Church in Humble, TX while the couple I moved with continued to search for the land they needed to start their ministry. In late 2005 they decided to move to Tennessee to pursue their ministry and we all agreed it would be best for me to stay in Houston. In early 2006 I was asked to lead the prayer ministries at the church in Humble and I quickly accepted. Shortly after that I met my wife at one of our prayer meetings. We were married in six months and ministering together at church, other local ministries and internationally.

Life was going great for me. I was married to a wonderful woman, held a leadership position at a prominent church and was establishing a profitable investment company. In 2007 I was working as a petroleum engineer for a company in Houston, TX but was also purchasing real estate and trading foreign currency.

My company became very prosperous so I chose to leave my position as an engineer and focus my efforts on my investment company. My wife and I also agreed that she would be able to leave her position as well. By mid-2008 the global credit crisis had left our finances in shambles and we found ourselves in a place of great despair.

This was very confusing to me because both my wife and I prayed and read our bible every day. We were tithe payers, served as the leaders of two prayer ministries and were going to other nations preaching the gospel and encouraging pastors and leaders. I remember wondering how something so devastating could happen to Christians so devoted to God's work.

I didn't understand why I found myself in that place because I thought good things happen to good people. I believed my devotion and service had allowed me to experience that level of blessing and there was no way I could lose what God had blessed me with if I continued down that path. After all I was living out my purpose; at least I thought I was.

Looking back now I can see that my situation was a result of my bad choices. At the time, these choices seemed to be the right ones. God had not failed on His end but I had failed on mine. In my pursuit for living out what I thought was my purpose I had somehow missed what I should have been pursuing; the presence of God.

Heaven on Earth

My loss was not caused by God's judgment nor do I feel I had to go through what I did to learn what I learned. My choices had gotten me in that mess but because the Father is so filled with love and mercy He chose to lead me to a place of restoration. He didn't scold me or punish me but took me by the hand and began to reveal to me a deeper revelation of His heart for my life.

The first scripture the Holy Spirit illuminated to me is Revelation 21:3-4. *And I heard a great voice out of heaven saying, "Behold, the tabernacle of God is with men, and he will dwell with them, and they shall be his people, and God himself shall be with them, and be their God. And God shall wipe away all tears from their eyes; and there shall be no more death, neither sorrow, nor crying, neither shall there be any more pain: for the former things are passed away".* As I read these verses I heard the Holy Spirit say to me that this promise was available to me now.

There is no sorrow, crying or pain in heaven and that dimension is available to us now. This was a thought I had pondered before but couldn't really put my hands on how it applied to my everyday life. I think the reason for this was because I had been taught that being to heavenly minded was no earthly good. Now I know the opposite to be true.

My conviction of this truth is found in the Gospel of Luke 11:1-2. *And it came to pass, that, as he was praying in a certain place, when he ceased, one of his disciples said unto him, Lord, teach us to pray, as John also taught his disciples. And he said unto them, When ye pray, say, Our Father which art in heaven, Hallowed be thy name. Thy kingdom come. Thy will be done, as in heaven, so in earth.* I find these verses quite striking because in them Jesus is revealing to us that the will of the Father is something we can discern.

Once we discern His will we are supposed to declare His Kingdom to come in the earth as it is in heaven. For every situation, there is a heavenly model that reveals God's Kingdom order. The implication here is that the earth can look like heaven if we discern the will of the Father and then bring His Kingdom order into the earth.

The Promise of Restoration

We have a promise of restoration when we experience loss. The next verses the Holy Spirit brought me to in this process were Proverbs 6:30-31. *Men do not despise a thief, if he steal to satisfy his soul when he is hungry; But if he be found, he shall restore sevenfold; he shall give all the substance of his house.* As I read these verses I heard the Holy Spirit say that if I would bring heaven into my circumstances then I would experience a sevenfold restoration. I would be given all the substance of the strong man who had come to steal, kill and destroy. I will be outlining the fullness of this process in later chapters but will say here that the first part, the sevenfold restoration, happened three years after I started pursuing God's presence.

After losing virtually everything, I had been seeking employment for nearly two years in the oil and gas industry but couldn't get a job. In late October of 2010 I received a phone call on a Wednesday night around 9:00 PM from a man who had seen my resume online. He was the operations manager for a petroleum engineering consulting firm located in Houston and my resume revealed that I was a good fit for what they were looking for.

At the time we were three months behind on mortgage payments, our refrigerator and cupboards were pretty much empty. We didn't know how we were going put food on the table let alone pay our other expenses. Growing up I remember similar circumstances but this was the first time in my adult life that I found myself in this type of predicament.

The next day I had a lunch meeting with the gentleman and by the time we had finished he offered me a job and said he was going to give me a sign on bonus. When I received the offer letter I was so excited I started yelling Hallelujah, Hallelujah!! The amount of the sign on bonus was enough to catch up our mortgage, fill our house with food, pay all the expenses we had at the time and put a down payment on a new vehicle I could drive to work.

Holy Spirit began to walk me through the restoration process in 2008 and by the end of 2011 I had received a sevenfold restoration of the salary that I left behind in 2007 when I left the oil and gas industry! Through this process of restoration Holy Spirit taught me about this ultimate partnership and how to access its fullness.

During this same time I started to regain a passion for praying for people in public places and telling them about Jesus. The fire that once burned on the inside started to reignite again. I started to see miracles happen when I would pray for people. There was something about pursuing an encounter with God in my personal time that was producing miracles around me.

The gifts of the Spirit were once again flowing regularly in my life rather than just occasionally. I started to move very profoundly in the gifts of knowledge, words of wisdom, prophecy, divers kinds of tongues and the interpretation of tongues. As amazing as this was to me I wanted more. People were experiencing healing when I prayed for them but not at the scale I was satisfied with.

When Jesus prayed people were healed. Not one person who came to Him left without experiencing His healing touch. He said that if I believed in Him then I could do the same works He did and greater. The miracles aren't my only measure of success but I have a passion to see Jesus's promise fulfilled in my life.

As I continually pursue God's presence year after year my businesses continue to grow as do the number of miracles that happen when I pray. As I pursue Him I become like Him and His purposes become a reality in my life. The void that once filled my heart is continually filled with peace and joy. His presence has become the pearl that I am willing to sell all in order to pursue and protect.

Passion for His Presence

King David, who is said to be man after God's own heart, seemed to have an unquenchable hunger for God's presence. Psalm 27, which was written by David, reveals this truth. *One thing have I desired of the LORD, that will I seek after; that I may dwell in the house of the LORD all the days of my life, to behold the beauty of the LORD, and to enquire in his temple.* He was a king with great wealth but to him nothing compared to what he experienced when he came into the presence of God. He had an appetite that could only be appeased by the one who formed him.

The heart of David is the mirror image of God's heart. Our Father desires to dwell with us all the days of our lives so that His beauty shines in our lives. One of the greatest joys and frustrations of being a parent is seeing our children begin to display our nature. We have great joy when we see them display our good qualities and frustration when we see them display our less than pleasant ones.

How much more joy does this give God when we begin to display His nature in our lives. He desires to be with us much more than we desire to be with Him. I believe this to be true even when we are doing everything in our power to desire Him. His passionate love for us displayed in the life of Jesus is so great that He was willing to endure the cross so we could be restored back to the place of continual communion.

This passionate desire is also displayed in Exodus 15:17 which says, *"Thou shalt bring them in, and plant them in the mountain of thine inheritance, in the place, O LORD, which thou hast made for thee to dwell in, in the Sanctuary, O Lord, which thy hands have established"*. God purposed in His heart to have a people in the earth He could dwell with.

The purpose of the Exodus out of Egypt was not to reach the promise land but to have an encounter with a loving Father who wanted to be with His children. The climax of the human experience is not reaching our proverbial promised land but it is experiencing the Father of Glory along the way.

Created for Intimacy to Bear God's Image

We are created for intimacy to bear God's image. This glorious experience was one of God's main purposes when He created mankind. He planted the celestial bodies in the skies and His words formed the majestic mountain peaks and the seemingly unending waters of the oceans. He called forth life from the seas and the earth and set them in their order. When it came time to create man He said, *"Let us make man in our image and after our likeness; and let them have dominion over the fish of the sea, and over the fowl of the air, and over the cattle, and over all the earth, and over every creeping thing that creepeth upon the earth"* (Genesis 1:26 KJV). God desired to have a partner here in the earth and it seemed good to Him to partner with one created in His image.

When our Father looked down upon His creation with much love and adoration He released to man the breath of life and suddenly everything changed. We don't have a clear record of the creation of the angels but up to this point there had never been such a creation. God was and is present within all things but only one thing was created to bear the fullness of His image; mankind.

Mankind was to be God's representative in the earth. He was to rule because of Him not instead of Him. He didn't choose to partner with the moon and the stars, the air, the land and the seas or the animals that filled them. He granted a partnership with those created in His image and gave them dominion over all His creation.

In Psalm 8 David wrote these words to the chief musician, "*When I consider thy heavens, the work of thy fingers, the moon and the stars, which thou hast ordained; What is man, that thou art mindful of him? and the son of man, that thou visitest him? For thou hast made him a little lower than Elohim, and hast crowned him with glory and honour*". This was not said of the angels, to be crowned with glory and honor. Only man was given this privilege.

God crowned mankind with the glory and honor of His image and placed him in the midst of a protected plush sanctuary towards the east in a place called Eden. The Hebrew for Eden is *aden*, which means luxury, pleasure or delight. This was a place of luxury where man was given the privilege to live sumptuously in peace.

Everywhere man looked he beheld the goodness and glory of his creator.

The environment and atmosphere of Eden was produced by God's presence in their midst. He had created this luxurious place and wanted to partner with man in order to watch over and steward it. It pleased the Fathers heart to have one created in His image looking after His affairs.

Created to Rule as God Rules

We were created in the image of the Father, to bear His image and multiply it wherever we find ourselves. His statements of creative purpose seen in the book of Genesis to the original Adam seem to hold this implication. *So God created man in his own image, in the image of God created he him; male and female created he them. And God blessed them, and God said unto them, Be fruitful, and multiply, and replenish the earth, and subdue it: and have dominion over the fish of the sea, and over the fowl of the air, and over every living thing that moveth upon the earth* (Genesis 1:27-28 KJV). With God's blessing came the anointing that would empower man to be fruitful and multiply; to replenish the earth and subdue it.

Man was to bear the fruit of God's image and allow it multiply so that it filled the whole earth. The apostle Paul revealed this to the church in Corinth when he said, *"But we all, with open face beholding as in a glass the glory of the Lord, are changed into the same image from glory to glory, even as by the Spirit of the Lord"* (2 Corinthians 3:18).

The apostle Peter revealed this truth in the second of his general epistles when he said, *"Grace and peace be multiplied unto you through the knowledge of God, and of Jesus our Lord, According as his divine power hath given unto us all things that pertain unto life and godliness, through the knowledge of him that hath called us to glory and virtue: Whereby are given unto us exceeding great and precious promises: that by these ye might be partakers of the divine nature, having escaped the corruption that is in the world through lust"* (2 Peter 1:4 KJV).

These verses seem to always fascinate me every time I read them. The fulfillment of the great and precious promises we are given through Christ is to be partakers of the divine nature. There is a place in God that allows us to see Him as if we are looking in a mirror. When we see Him we are transformed into His image by Holy Spirit.

Jesus modeled this way of life for us so beautifully. He came in the image of the father empowered by Holy Spirit to be the firstborn of a people who would embrace the Fathers invitation to partner with Him. It is my conviction that every plan and purpose of God revolves around this simple but powerful principle that I call the ultimate partnership. There is no greater privilege than to be the ones whom God has chosen to entrust His Spirit. Neither is there any greater responsibility.

Chapter 2

Crowned with Glory and Honor

Our story begins with man being crowned with the glory and honor of bearing God's image. As I stated earlier, Adam and Eve were placed in the midst of a protected plush sanctuary towards the east in a place called Eden. This was a place of luxury where man was given the privilege to live sumptuously in peace.

The environment and atmosphere of Eden was produced by God's presence. He had created this luxurious place and wanted to partner with man in order to watch over and steward it as we see in Genesis 2:15. *And the LORD God took the man, and put him into the garden of Eden to dress it and to keep it.*

On face value this may seem like it was a menial task; to be crowned with glory and honor to be Gods gardener. This of course was not some menial task to keep Adam and Eve busy. God was creating the perfect environment where His blessings upon them could grow into maturity as they communed with Him in His presence day by day.

Man and woman were created in the image of God to rule over the earth and to be His representatives. They were destined to represent Him as ambassadors in personality and function. Genesis 1:27-28 says, *"So God created man in his own image, in the image of God created he him; male and female created he them. And God blessed them, and God said unto them, Be fruitful, and multiply, and replenish the earth, and subdue it: and have dominion over the fish of the sea, and over the fowl of the air, and over every living thing that moveth upon the earth"*.

Dominion: Crowned with Authority

When God's blessing was released upon mankind the authority to rule over the affairs of the earth was awakened and released. When He said, *"Be fruitful, and multiply, and replenish the earth, and subdue it"* He was not merely giving a commandment to be obeyed. He was awakening within man His creative purposes and releasing to them the ability to be what He was speaking; fruitful in His image.

Every individual has within them the ability to awaken God's authority because it is a part of our creative purpose. We were created to rule or have dominion. Those of you who are parents would agree that this intrinsic property is easily seen in your children. At a very early age they just realize they have their own will and they have no problem imposing it on others and their environment.

Dominion was Gods initial intent for man and a protected plush sanctuary filled with His presence was the ideal environment for this responsibility to be perfected.

The Hebrew word for dominion used in Genesis 1:26 is *radah*, which means to rule, to dominate, to tread down, to cause to dominate.

When taken in the context of the text, dominion is written with the understanding that the ability to rule as God rules is not intrinsic. It is more perfectly stated as he or she rules, dominates, treads down or is caused to dominate. Adam and Eve were given the responsibility to rule but their ability to do so properly was not found within themselves; they were to rule as God rules.

Mankind was designed to rule because of God and not instead of Him. His style of leadership is much different than we see in many areas of our society today. His way of ruling is never to impose His will but to create a safe environment of empowerment where people are given the opportunity to partner with Him. Only then is man able to reach the fullness of his potential.

Adam and Eve and all of mankind after them were to represent God in the earth as His governing body. As I stated in the last paragraph, their position was not given or granted to rule instead of God but because of His design. Their effectiveness to carry out this assignment depended totally on their partnership with Him. He came to walk and talk with them in the cool of the day. Their ability to live and rule effectively came as a result of these afternoon walks with their Father.

Dominion: The Result of God's Blessing

God's delegated authority upon our lives is a result of His blessing upon us. The Hebrew words used in

Genesis 1:28 for "God blessed" are *Elohim barak*. This reveals to us that our Creator kneeled down as He spoke over us His creative purposes. I believe this gives us the picture of the process of Him kneeling down and breathing within us His breath of life.

With that one breath, we received all the fullness of God's blessing. Many view blessing as material prosperity. Others view it as physical and emotional health. Though all of these are byproducts of His blessing upon us they do not capture its fullness. Blessing is His anointing that allows us to increase, prosper and multiply all that is good in our lives as we are transformed into the image of His glory.

The very first thing the eyes of man looked upon was the face and the stature of His creator. As God was kneeling over him He was not only bringing life to His creation but was allowing him to see what he should look like. In essence He was saying to mankind, "I created you and I have imprinted myself within your being". As He kneeled over us and breathed into us His breath of life, His *barak* (blessing) initiated our ability to rule effectively.

When Adam became aware of himself through his senses he also became aware of his purpose as he stared in the passionate eyes of his Father. As God was kneeling over him breathing into him, He was releasing the ability to be fruitful, to multiply, to replenish, to subdue and to have dominion. He was showing him the image of glory that would become his blueprint for life.

Some are unable to live in the fullness of this promise because they are unaware they possess this ability. Others are very aware of it but are unable to live in true dominion because their image of ruling does not look like Gods. We must commune with His presence every day in order to enter into the fullness of His blessings.

Be Fruitful and Multiply

God's first statement of creative purpose was, "Be fruitful and multiply". So what was he really saying? Was He commanding us to produce fruit and lots of it or reproduce offspring? The Hebrew for "God said be fruitful and multiply" is *Elohim amar parah rabah*. This phrase is better translated as God called it to bear and be increased.

With this statement, God wasn't telling them to produce something from the sense of planting seed or cultivating behavior. On this occasion He was speaking His creative purpose as He blessed them. Once these words were spoken, mankind had the ability to bear His image and to be multiplied and increased in bearing His image.

The implication of increasing and multiplying as we bear God's image is rather interesting to me. Though the earth was and is filled with God, it was missing His image. The scriptures have many comparisons in which God is compared to creation so we can come to know Him but we are the only creation designed to bear His image. Not only are we chosen to bear His image but to multiply His image in the earth so that it is increased.

God's statement is definitely relating to reproduction but in a way that establishes His image and causes it to increase. Another implication here is that we were designed to continually increase. This is a principle of the Kingdom of God that we will talk about in great detail later but its implication is seen in our beginning. Any notion of us diminishing as a people is just not God's plan. We are created to increase and to continue to increase.

Replenish and Subdue the Earth

The next phrase of God's blessing was, "Replenish the earth and subdue it". This statement in Hebrew is *male' erets kabash,* which is better translated to say, "Consecrate the earth and establish My image in it so that it overflows with My abundance". Consecration is the process by which something is set apart for a specific purpose. The earth was created and set apart as our dwelling place.

The first implication here is that it is our responsibility to bring heavens rule into our dwelling place so that it overflows with God's abundance. By possessing the ability to bear God's image we are able to rule the way He does. As we are multiplied and increased in bearing His image all of our surroundings begin to burst forth and overflow with abundance.

Another implication in this statement is that the earth did not reflect God's perfect order at the time Adam and Eve were created. Had His order been present throughout the earth there would be nothing to subdue and it would not need to be replenished with His abundance. We will delve much deeper into this thought later but it is obvious to me that satan was present at this time brining disorder and chaos.

Delegated Authority

God created all things for His pleasure. He looked at everything He made and said that it was good. Though this is true the way He interacted with man was different than all the rest of His creation. Rather than just speak him into existence like He did with the rest of creation He took His time and formed him from the dust of the earth. It was close and personal, revealing to him the blessing of being made in His image. We catch a glimpse of this relationship in Genesis 2:19 which says, *"And out of the ground the LORD God formed every beast of the field, and every fowl of the air; and brought them unto Adam to see what he would call them: and whatsoever Adam called every living creature, that was the name thereof".*

This interaction between God and Adam is astonishing to me. I can almost picture them as they survey each animal and then come to an agreement as to which name best defines their purpose. Names are filled with purpose and destiny biblically and God was allowing Adam to determine the purpose and destiny of every animal. I believe this is the first time man began to move in his delegated authority over creation to unlock its potential.

Adam was being unveiled to creation as bearing God's image. He was being increased in that image with each passing animal. He was consecrating each one so that they would overflow with God's creative purposes. This reveals the heart of God in such a beautiful way with regard to man. We were not created to be like robots but to be co-laborers working alongside Him.

There are many who go to war over the ownership of land but mankind was not given the earth to rule as their possession. We were to be in partnership with God and establish His rule His way. Psalm 115:16 says, *"The heaven, even the heavens, are the LORD'S: but the earth hath he given to the children of men"*. The phrase "hath he given" here does not mean a transfer of ownership but to assign or to appoint.

The writer of Psalm 115 is revealing to us that the LORD rules in the heavens and He has assigned the earth to all mankind. His breath of life awakened us to our creative purpose; to rule in the earth as He rules. It is my conviction that most, if not all, of the events, both good and bad, which take place on this earth, are a result of how man has exercised his delegated authority; not as a result of God's sovereignty.

As you can see we have a very significant role to play and God's delegated authority is not something to take lightly. We have a great responsibility to ensure the affairs of our garden are being conducted according to God's ways so that it overflows with His abundance. Understanding how this flow of authority operates is a great source of power to bring heaven into the earth when exercised properly.

Chapter 3

The Transfer of Authority

I have often wondered and pondered the Garden and its placement. The Hebrew word for garden used in Genesis chapter two is *gan*, which means an enclosure. This word paints the picture of a garden that has been fenced in with trees and shrubbery as if to shield it from any outside influence.

Man was placed in this protected place and instructed to dress it and keep it (See Genesis 2:15). The Hebrew words for tend and keep that are used in the text are *abad* and *shamar*, which mean to work and to guard. Man was placed in the garden to co-labor and was instructed to guard it.

Adam and Eve were commanded to tend and guard this protected plush sanctuary. Ultimately the goal was to establish and maintain God's order where they had been placed and then allow this same order to be increased and multiply until it covered the entire earth. They were told to guard this place but to guard it from what?

We really don't see much in the text that reveals to us any danger until we get to Genesis 3:1. *Now the serpent was more subtle than any beast of the field which the LORD God had made. And he said unto the woman, Yea, hath God said, Ye shall not eat of every tree of the garden?* Out of nowhere a talking serpent appears that is described as being more subtle than any beast of the field.

The implication here is that outside of this hedged in place the order of things was different than inside of it. The devil was already here on the earth attempting to establish his order and the garden was his prize. We see this illustrated as the serpent enters the scene to reveal to Eve a different way of thinking.

Satan's Fall

Revelation 12:4 describes a dragon being cast down to the earth taking one third of the stars with it. This may be making reference to fall of satan and his excommunication from Heaven. The prophet Isaiah also describes a similar scene in Isaiah 14:12-14. *How art thou fallen from heaven, O Lucifer, son of the morning! How art thou cut down to the ground, which didst weaken the nations! For thou hast said in thine heart, I will ascend into heaven, I will exalt my throne above the stars of God: I will sit also upon the mount of the congregation, in the sides of the north: I will ascend above the heights of the clouds; I will be like the most High.*

Lucifer, who was the son of the morning, lost his place in heaven because of his pride and arrogance. He desired to be worshiped by the entire heavenly host and wanted to direct all the affairs of men like the most High.

His clothing was made of precious stones and within him was a tambourine.

He was appointed as the covering cherub watching over the glory of God in His holy mountain (See Ezekiel 28:13-14). He was perfect in all his ways until something within him said that he could be the one to be desired. Ezekiel 28:17 says, *"Thine heart was lifted up because of thy beauty, thou hast corrupted thy wisdom by reason of thy brightness: I will cast thee to the ground, I will lay thee before kings, that they may behold thee"*.

The point here is to recognize that satan was already here in the earth attempting to establish his order before God made Adam and Eve and placed them in the midst of the garden. God created a place overflowing with His goodness and perfect order in the midst of satan's domain. This must have been infuriating and frustrating to him knowing that he had no ability to stop what was happening.

God created a protected place shielded from satan's disorder and chaos. I believe He did this so those created in His image would be able to grow into maturity and then establish His order in the entire earth. The garden was the womb by which man would be nurtured and protected so that he could be increased and multiplied in God's image until His glory filled the entire earth.

There is No Struggle Between Good and Evil

Satan has never been a threat to God. He was and is the created and not the creator. God is infinite in power and authority. Satan may have been clothed with precious stones but God is beauty and honor, majesty and infinite strength. His brightness penetrates and displaces all darkness and it cannot be overshadowed.

Throughout history philosophers have portrayed satan as God's equal. He has been portrayed as an adversary who could challenge God's authority in an epic battle of good against evil. This ideology is quite laughable and its source comes from the one who would like to exalt himself above God's throne. There has never been a battle between God and satan and he has never been nor will he ever be an equal adversary to God.

The truth of the matter is that God could have annihilated satan and all those who followed him in a moment but he chose to handle him differently. He chose to deal with this deceiver by empowering the ones made in His image, those who would choose to worship Him. What a brilliant way to handle this situation.

Satan wanted to be worshiped as God so God chose to defeat him with the issue of his rebellion. This was not God's plan for him but in arrogance he chose to take matters into his own hands. It's rather difficult for me to see how satan thought he could pull it off but he obviously did. This selfish narcissistic expression of self will cost him his place before God and brought down one third of the angels with him.

Equipped for Battle in His Presence

We don't see a record of Adam and Eve receiving any detailed instructions as to how to tend the garden or how to deal with this serpent that had made his way into their domain. There were no schools of prayer to teach them how to plead the blood of Jesus. We don't see God informing them to pray in the Spirit or the name of Jesus to cast the devil out.

Today there are thousands of books on spiritual warfare and I am thankful for that but it seemed all Adam and Eve needed to guard their domain was the presence of God that saturated their atmosphere. The only instructions they were given are seen in Genesis 2:16-17. *And the LORD God commanded the man, saying, "Of every tree of the garden thou mayest freely eat: But of the tree of the knowledge of good and evil, thou shalt not eat of it: for in the day that thou eatest thereof thou shalt surely die".*

Adam and Eve received all the instruction and empowerment they needed as the Lord dwelt among them. As they spent time in His presence, in this place of intimacy with God all their needs were met. I believe as they communed with Him in the cool of the day He was showing them how to deal with the serpent.

We see this illustrated by David who said, *"The LORD is my shepherd; I shall not want. He makes me lie down in green pastures. He leads me beside still waters. He restores my soul. He leads me in paths of righteousness for his name's sake. Even though I walk through the valley of the shadow of death, I will fear no evil, for you are with me; your rod and your staff, they comfort me. You prepare a table before me in the presence of my enemies; you anoint my head with oil; my cup overflows. Surely goodness and mercy shall follow me all the days of my life, and I shall dwell in the house of the LORD forever".* (Psalm 23 NKJV)

As we abide in His presence He restores our soul, leads us in paths of righteousness and prepares a table for us in the midst of our enemies. Much of what is taught today in regards to spiritual warfare puts too much emphasis on our adversary in my opinion. Many schools of thought seem to be tempered using Sun Tzo's book The Art of War.

The apostle Paul does encourage us to be aware of the enemies devises in 2 Corinthians 2:11 but Sun Tzo's ideologies fall tragically short of how God views warfare. Our weapons are mighty through Christ to pull down strong holds. We are to put on His armor so that we can stand against the weapons of the enemy. Christ Jesus, who came to reveal the Father, is our armor and our weapon.

God prepares a table for us in the midst of our enemies. As we come to dine with our Father no enemy can overtake us whether we understand his tactics or not. As we live by faith we are established and as we stand firm on the words of His prophets we prosper. When we worship Him and sing praises to His name He sends out a network of warring angels on our behalf (See 2 Chronicles 20:20-22). The failure in the garden was not due to a lack of instruction but it was due to a change of focus.

The Change in Focus

When the serpent approached Eve he knew that he couldn't come in with guns blazing. He knew they were equipped with the power and authority to deal with him. He did not have the authority to take the garden and establish his rule by force. If he was going to achieve his goal he would need to find a way to convince Adam and

Eve to transfer over the title deed of what God had given them.

He approached Eve and posed a simple question, *Did God actually say, "You shall not eat of any tree in the garden?"* (See Genesis 3:1) When we look at how he asked this question it seems to me that the serpent didn't know what God had told them. It's as if he was fishing for a way to deceive her.

Eve answers the serpant and says, *"We may eat of the fruit of the trees in the garden, but God said, "You shall not eat of the fruit of the tree that is in the midst of the garden, neither shall you touch it, lest you die".* In answering him she revealed to him how he could shift her focus. He goes on to propose to her that she wouldn't die but would actually become like God knowing good and evil (See Genesis 3:3-5).

The serpent had convinced Eve that God had been holding out on her and was able to shift her desires. They were already created in God's image. Prior to this conversation what they had was sufficient. They had plenty of food to fill their bellies but more importantly they had the presence of God to fill their soul and spirit.

When Eve looked at the tree of the knowledge of good and evil after her conversation with the serpent she didn't see something that would cause her to perish. She saw something that would fulfill her natural and emotional appetites. In essence she saw what the serpent told her; something that could make her like God.

I find this to be quite interesting because they were already like God. They were created in His image and had been given dominion over all they could see. Obviously they didn't need to have the knowledge of good and evil to accomplish what they were created to do at this time because God had withheld it from them. We really don't know why He did this but we do know that what He had provided was sufficient.

Adams Failure

There has been much talk about Eve's failure in the garden but the real failure came when Adam transgressed. I believe that if Adam would have fulfilled God's commandment our world would be a much different place today. Her failure is not what caused them to be deported out of their sanctuary of protection but it was Adams.

This truth is revealed in Romans 5:14 which says, *"Nevertheless death reigned from Adam to Moses, even over them that had not sinned after the similitude of Adam's transgression, who is the figure of him that was to come"*. Two verses earlier the apostle Paul uses the Greek word anthropos, which means mankind in general. If this word was used here as well then we could not say it was Adam but he specifically calls him by name. He reveals that it was Adams transgression that caused sin to reign.

After they ate the fruit a new emotion entered their world that they had never felt before. When they looked at one another's nakedness they were afraid and they covered themselves with fig leaves. Their outlook on their environment had totally changed. The peace and protection they had enjoyed up to this point seemed to be gone.

When they heard God in the evening coming to be with them they hid themselves from His presence. Adam's transgression was not only that he ate the fruit he was forbidden to eat but he failed to rule his environment and then hid himself from God's presence. Outside of God's presence he would not be able to rule effectively.

When Adam failed to maintain God's rule in the garden he transferred his authority to the serpent, whose words he was in agreement with. He was no longer seeing clearly even though satan had convinced them that their eyes would be opened to see what God had kept from them. Prior to this failure he was not afraid of God or anything else in the garden.

Adams choice affected his ability to live by faith from the place of intimacy in God's presence. In essence the disorder that was found outside the garden had made its way into the garden. This was not God's plan. Adam was not supposed to rule being influenced by the one who was cast out of heaven. Mankind was destined to rule as God rules being influenced by His goodness as he remained in the intimate place of His presence.

Man Under the Yoke of Sin

As a result of this new found awareness the seed of man became sinful. A demonstration of this can be seen in the first offspring that Adam and Eve produced outside of the Garden; Cain and Able. In Genesis 4:8 we read the first historical account of premeditated murder.

Out of jealousy Cain murdered his brother in the field. Because Adam had violated God's commandment and hid himself from His presence the result was the shedding of innocent blood in the next generation. Man was being fruitful and multiplying and replenishing the earth but it was not as God had intended.

The farther away man moved from God's presence the more sinful his nature became. Man continued to increase and multiply but not as God intended. Genesis 6 reveals a generation of mighty men whose imaginations lusted after evil continually. Satan's plan seemed to be unstoppable as there was great wickedness in the earth.

God saw how men were conducting themselves and His heart was grieved. The ones who were created to be in communion with Him seemed to have no interest in cultivating that relationship. However in the midst of all this wickedness there was a man whose heart was pure; Noah. As long as there is one individual willing to find his way back into God's presence His plan will always prevail.

Some have proposed that the fall of Adam took away our ability to go to heaven and I agree. But as we can see we lost much more than that. We lost our ability to fulfill our purpose in the earth. We were created for intimacy; to rule in the earth as God rules from the place of His presence. The fall took us out of this place of communion and intimacy with God leaving us to our devises.

Even though our condition was dire God had a plan to restore us. *And the LORD God said unto the serpent, "Because thou hast done this, thou art cursed above all cattle, and above every beast of the field; upon thy belly shalt thou go, and dust shalt thou eat all the days of thy life: I will put enmity between thee and the woman, and between thy seed and her seed; it shall bruise thy head, and thou shalt bruise his heel*' (Genesis 3:14-15). In this decree God makes it very clear that satan's rule was going to be only for a season. A time would come when the seed of a woman would crush his headship.

Chapter 4

The Beginning of Restoration

Time pressed on for sixty six generations after the time of Noah and then something changed. A man named John began to preach in the wilderness declaring that he was sent to witness the coming of the Son of God. At the same time the Jews were selecting the Passover lamb that would be offered at the coming feast He came; the Lamb of God, the King of kings, the Lord of lords, Immanuel, God with us. John proclaimed, "Behold the Lamb of God who takes away the sin of the world" (See John 1:29)

Jesus came to the earth for a number of reasons. He was the Lamb of God come to take away sin but he was also the "seed of the woman" come to take care of some unfinished business. *He that committeth sin is of the devil; for the devil sinneth from the beginning. For this purpose the Son of God was manifested, that he might destroy the works of the devil* (1 John 3:8).

One of Jesus's primary assignments was to destroy the works of the Devil, which are sin and death. This included rescuing mankind from his fallen state and restoring back to him his authority to rule (See Luke 19:10). He came with the full power and authority of the Father, demonstrating His goodness to a lost and dying world.

Satan's Plot

Satan has a history of trying to stop God's plan from coming into fullness. He was the inspiration behind the plot to kill all the new born sons in Egypt during the time Moses was born (See Exodus 1:16-22). He is not omniscient like God who knows all things, so he must have heard the people crying out for a deliverer knowing that God would answer. I am certain that his actions were inspired by fear as he knew one would be coming who would have the ability to not only liberate the children of Israel but all mankind. He just didn't know when.

As time went on the prophets began to reveal the signs of His coming. When the time was fulfilled he was born in the city of Bethlehem just as the prophet Micah had predicted. *But you, O Bethlehem Ephrathah, who are too little to be among the clans of Judah, from you shall come forth for me one who is to be ruler in Israel, whose coming forth is from of old, from ancient days* (Micah 5:2).

Wise men came from the east to Jerusalem asking where they could find the King of the Jews. They said they had seen His star in the east and had come to worship Him. These men must have been aware of the prophecy of Balaam; a Gentile prophet who was hired by Balak the king of the Moabites to curse God's people after they came out of Egypt (See Numbers 22:4-5). He saw in a vision a star arising, revealing the one who was coming with dominion (See Numbers 24:17-19).

There coming caused quite an uproar in the city of Jerusalem as Herod, the Roman emperor, scrambled to find where this King was to be born. Once the Jews had revealed to him the location of Jesus's birth according to Micah's prophesy satan once again inspired a mass genocide of innocent children in an attempt to stop this deliverer from coming.

The devil was of course unsuccessful as God directed Mary and Joseph to take Jesus to Egypt until this season ended. We really don't know if the devil thought he was successful but I can only imagine the look in his eyes when he heard the voice of John the Baptist proclaim, *"Prepare the way of the Lord and make His paths straight"* (See Mark 1:3).

The Plot Thickens

Knowing that he was unsuccessful some thirty years earlier he must have been scrambling to come up with a plan to keep his empire from falling. He was preparing for a confrontation but God was ready to initiate one. After Jesus was baptized in the Jordan River the heavens opened and Holy Spirit descended upon Him as God declared, *"This is my beloved Son in whom I am well pleased"*.

After this moment of affirmation, Jesus was led into the wilderness by Holy Spirit to be tempted by the devil. For many the devil is someone to be feared but for Jesus he was a slithery serpent running for his life knowing he was about to be crushed under His feet. I can only imagine the anticipation as He made His way into the wilderness.

Jesus had been waiting some three thousand years for this moment and now finally the time came to deal with this deceiver. After enduring a forty day fast the devil shows up and tries the same strategy that was successful in the garden. Let's take a look at the Gospel of Matthew to see how this played out.

> *And the tempter came and said to him, "If you are the Son of God, command these stones to become loaves of bread." But he answered, "It is written, "'Man shall not live by bread alone, but by every word that comes from the mouth of God.'" Then the devil took him to the holy city and set him on the pinnacle of the temple and said to him, "If you are the Son of God, throw yourself down, for it is written, "'He will command his angels concerning you,' and "On their hands they will bear you up, lest you strike your foot against a stone." Jesus said to him, "Again it is written, 'You shall not put the Lord your God to the test.'" Again, the devil took him to a very high mountain and showed him all the kingdoms of the world and their glory. And he said to him, "All these I will give you, if you will fall down and worship me." Then Jesus said to him, "Be gone, satan! For it is written, "'You shall worship the Lord your God and him only shall you serve.'" Then the devil left him, and behold, angels came and were ministering to him* (Matthew 4:3-11).

Our restoration began with this confrontation in the wilderness, of which satan had no chance in winning. Traditional theologians say that these temptations can be described as the lust of the flesh, the lust of the eye and the pride of life. Though this may have some merit the only real challenge satan was posing to Jesus was whether or not He was the Son of God.

Once satan realized that Jesus was the one sent to destroy him by the way He responded to his questions all he could do is offer Him what He came to take back; the kingdoms of the earth and their glory. This was the same tactic he used in the garden; to offer something that was already rightfully His at the expense of worship.

Luke's account of the temptation reveals to us a slightly different picture. *And the devil, taking him up into an high mountain, shewed unto him all the kingdoms of the world in a moment of time. And the devil said unto him, All this power will I give thee, and the glory of them: for that is delivered unto me; and to whomsoever I will I give it. If thou therefore wilt worship me, all shall be thine* (Luke 4:6-8). The Greek word for power here is *exousia,* which is better translated as authority.

Satan was arrogantly boasting of the authority and the glory he had stolen from mankind. To me this appears to be an attempt by the devil to impress on Jesus that he was worthy of His worship. But he was in for a rude awakening. In this moment of time, all the authority and the glory that satan had stolen now rested upon its rightful owner; Jesus the Son of God and the Son of Man.

His Kingdom Has Come

After being baptized in the Jordan River something about Jesus changed. Those who witnessed the Spirit descend upon Him and heard the voice of the Father reverberate through the atmosphere as He revealed His son to the world must have been in awe. This son of a carpenter from Nazareth was actually the Son of God; the Messiah the prophets had spoken of for centuries.

With one statement, Jesus announced to the world that the restoration of all things had begun after overcoming the devil in the wilderness. *From that time Jesus began to preach and to say, "Repent, for the kingdom of heaven is at hand"*(Matthew 4:17). This was an unprecedented statement that the heavens and the earth had been waiting to hear. Finally the promise that God made to the serpent some three thousand years earlier was manifesting before his eyes (See Genesis 3:15).

From this point on Jesus continued to reveal the Kingdom of Heaven everywhere He went. Every action and every miracle revealed this Kingdom that would destroy the works of the devil. As He traveled throughout the land of Israel lepers were cleansed, the blind regained their sight, those possessed by demons were delivered, people were raised from the dead and many were healed of sicknesses and infirmities. The undeniable fruits of the Kingdom shook the world as satan's headship was being crushed.

As Jesus's disciples walked with Him, they were amazed at His demonstration of power. One such occasion is seen in the Gospels of Matthew, Mark and Luke where Jesus rebukes the wind and the seas in the middle of a storm after being awakened by His disciples. *And he saith unto them, "Why are ye fearful, O ye of little faith?" Then he arose, and rebuked the winds and the sea; and there was a great calm. But the men marvelled, saying, "What manner of man is this, that even the winds and the sea obey him!"* (Matthew 8:26-27).

Many of the Jews alive during this generation believed that Jesus had come to overthrow the Roman

Empire and become the king who would lead them back into glory. The miracles that followed Him seemed to reaffirm this way of thinking but when He came into the earth His agenda was not political. He came to destroy the works of the devil and then enable us to do the same as we partner with Him. His kingdom is not a political one to enable God's people to rule over all the other people of the world but to give access to all mankind the opportunity to experience a life filled with God's blessing and abundance.

Chapter 5

The Kingdom is at Hand

Throughout history many kingdoms have risen to power and made their mark on humanity. Some were known for great military power. Others were known for great technological innovation. Many of our modern conveniences and forms of human government find their genesis in these ancient kingdoms that once thrived. Though many historical kingdoms have influenced our daily lives no other kingdom changed the history of mankind more than the one John the Baptist declared and Jesus demonstrated.

The Greek word for "kingdom" found in the Gospels is basileia. This is the only word used in the New Testament to describe the Kingdom of Heaven. Basileia means royal power, kingship, dominion or to rule. Strong's Greek lexicon states that "this word is not to be confused with an actual physical kingdom but rather the right or authority to rule over a kingdom". It is derived from a Greek word that means to walk, through the concept of a foundation of power.

This Kingdom that Jesus demonstrated is best defined as the sovereign government of God that is the source of all things in heaven and earth; having the Lord Jesus Christ as the sovereign head, the angelic host as its administering body in the heavens and the Church as its administering body in the earth being empowered by Holy Spirit. The Kingdom of Heaven is not a physical kingdom established by men but it is the royal power or authority given to Jesus by the Father.

The same authority given to Jesus is given to those who believe in Him. When Jesus spoke of the Kingdom of Heaven in the scriptures He was speaking directly of the royal power of Himself as the triumphant Messiah and the royal power and dignity conferred on those who function in His domain by faith. As ambassadors of God's kingdom we are empowered by the Holy Spirit to rule in the earth as God rules in the heavens.

A Kingdom of Love and Power

The Kingdom of Heaven is not an earthly kingdom even though it manifests and functions in the earth. It is our right or authority that enables us to bring heaven into every earthly kingdom so that it reflects heaven's reality. This royal power is given to us by Jesus who sends Holy Spirit to enable us to walk in power and victory in the earth as He did. We were created for intimacy to rule in the earth as He rules in the heavens.

The Kingdom of Heaven is a kingdom of love and power. It is designed by God to enable us to walk in love and power the way Jesus did. The gospel of Matthew gives us a glimpse of this truth. *And Jesus went about all the cities and villages, teaching in their synagogues, and preaching the gospel of the kingdom, and healing every sickness and every disease among the people* (Matthew 9:35). Everywhere Jesus went declaring His kingdom people were healed of sickness and liberated from the devils kingdom of oppression.

The apostle John understood this very well. He defined God as love two times in his first general epistle (see 1 John 4:8; 4:16). The Father is love and therefore His Kingdom is motivated by love. It is this foundation that energizes faith releasing heaven into earth. As faith works through love the miraculous becomes easily actualized (see Galatians 5:6). The kingdoms of this world, along with the prince of this world, have no power against the Father's demonstration of love working through faith.

The Kingdom Seed

The working of the Father's love in those who embrace His Kingdom by faith begins in seed form. Matthew's Gospel reveals to us many parables that Jesus used to expound on how His kingdom functions but I would like to focus on only one. *Another parable put He forth unto them, saying, "The kingdom of heaven is like to a grain of mustard seed, which a man took, and sowed in his field; Which indeed is the least of all seeds: but when it is grown, it is the greatest among herbs, and becometh a tree, so that the birds of the air come and lodge in the branches thereof"* (Mathew 13:31-32). This verse is quite perplexing at first. How can something so great be like something that is so small?

The Kingdom of Heaven is like a grain of mustard seed that is sown into a field. According to Jesus this Kingdom seed is the least of all seeds. It's an amazing thought to think that the least of all seeds would have the ability to produce something that is described as being the greatest. The Greek here is *spermah*, which means something sown. It can also mean offspring or a remnant that has been kept over for planting. The Kingdom seed is specifically selected as a remnant from the harvest to be sown into the field that possesses the ability to become the greatest.

According to Jesus, the Kingdom of Heaven is like the least of all seeds but grows into the greatest of all herbs. In making this statement, I believe He was trying to direct our attention to the intrinsic properties of the Kingdom. We must take this statement both qualitatively and quantitatively. Jesus was not just bringing our attention to the size of the seed to show that it was small, but He was also bringing our attention to the fact that it was not sought after like other seeds.

In Jesus' time in the region where he lived, the mustard seed was not sought after like other seeds because it could not be grown in smaller gardens. When full grown it reached heights of nine feet tall and had branches with a very wide span. Anyone who planted a mustard seed in their personal garden could plan on having a tree that overshadowed everything else planted.

Even though this seed was not the most desirable in terms of its apparent value, once it grew it became the greatest among herbs. Jesus was trying to draw our attention to the quality of the DNA inside the seed. Even though this seed is very small in size and not desired by the masses, it has within it the DNA to produce something great when full grown.

The Kingdom of Heaven begins as the least both in size and desire but it becomes the greatest. Once the Kingdom seed is sown into an individual, family, region or nation, it becomes the prevailing force that shapes that individual, family, region or nation as long as the conditions are conducive for its growth to maturity. The partnership between the seed, the sower and the one who receives it creates the potential for Heaven to come into earth.

Jesus illustrated this Kingdom seed principle in the parable of the sower to a large audience of listeners near sea of Gallilee. *On the same day Jesus went out of the house and sat by the sea. And great multitudes were gathered together to Him, so that He got into a boat and sat; and the whole multitude stood on the shore. Then He spoke many things to them in parables, saying: "Behold, a sower went out to sow. And as he sowed, some seed fell by the wayside; and the birds came and devoured them. Some fell on stony places, where they did not have much earth; and they immediately sprang up because they had no depth of earth. But when the sun was up they were scorched, and because they had no root they withered away. And some fell among thorns, and the thorns sprang up and choked them. But others fell on good ground and yielded a crop: some a hundredfold, some sixty, some thirty. He who has ears to hear, let him hear!"* (Matthew 13:1-9 ASV).

The Father designed His Kingdom in such a way that it requires partnership and agreement to function properly. In order to bring the Kingdom of Heaven into the earth, there must be someone willing to go as a sower. The sower partners with Heaven and releases an opportunity for a Kingdom harvest. Those who are given the opportunity to experience Heavens authority must fully agree with its DNA to see the harvest come into its fullness. When this happens the fruit of the Kingdom seed produces righteousness, peace and joy in Holy Spirit (see Romans 14:17).

The Greatest Kingdom

Jesus continually illustrated and demonstrated to all that followed and opposed Him that the Kingdom of Heaven truly is the greatest. As He walked the earth partnering with heaven, sickness and disease were no threat to His message of the Kingdom. Demons would cry out in His presence asking for mercy. The religious leaders could not confound His wisdom and the political system could not stop His coming.

Jesus came to display to all the Kingdom of Heaven by casting out devils, cleansing lepers, raising the dead and healing the sick and all that were oppressed by the devil. Many believed that He had come to establish a political system that would overthrow the Roman Empire. As such, many in Israel were waiting for Him to liberate them from Rome's reign of tyranny. Instead He came to do so much more; to liberate the world from the kingdom of darkness and destroy the works of the devil.

The kingdom that Jesus declared is greater than every earthly kingdom. It is the reservoir that feeds every nation, royal family, corporation or government. No kingdom in existence today has been established by its own intrinsic power. In Romans 13:1 the apostle Paul says, *"There is no power but of God: the powers that be are ordained of God"*. The company we work for is not our source; the US Government is not our source, nor is any insurance company, medical facility or any other institution. The Kingdom of God is our source and God uses all these things in the earth to perform His will.

Wherever we find ourselves we can partner with heaven and have access to all of heavens resources. We are not limited by the impossible. *Jesus said unto him, If thou canst believe, all things are possible to him that believeth* (Mark 9:23). This is an amazing promise that allows us to find great security in a Kingdom that is far greater than any other system of authority.

Chapter 6

The Father's Sovereign Government

The Father's Sovereign Government is already so large that it encompasses the entire universe. However, the time is coming when it will envelope every earthly kingdom. It begins as a seed but continues to expand until it becomes the dominant force. The prophet Isaiah saw this by revelation when he said, *"Of the increase of His government and peace there will be no end, upon the throne of David and over His kingdom, to order it and establish it with judgment and justice from that time forward, even forever. The zeal of the LORD of hosts will perform this"* (Isaiah 9:7).

There is much debate in our culture about God's sovereignty. The Father is sovereign, which means He is all powerful and can do anything at any time. In most cases, this fact is not the subject of debate but how His sovereignty operates is. In His sovereignty, He sets the order of what is to be established in the heavens and in the earth (see Acts 17:24-26). The Father has predetermined according to His own will and power what He wants to do and when He wants to do it. It is however foolish to think that because He has a predetermined will that it is always accomplished.

There are many who view the Father's sovereignty in a way that diminishes His goodness. For example cessation theology teaches that miracles are a result of

God's sovereignty. This theology states that sometimes God desires to heal and other times He doesn't. Jesus, who came in the image of the Father to reveal His will, never turned anyone away who came to Him for healing. All that came to Him seeking a miracle were healed, liberated and filled with the Father's goodness. This reveals to us that there is not an occasion where God is not willing to heal.

The Father is sovereign and His sovereignty flows through the Kingdom but not without partnership and agreement. The Kingdom of Heaven is not a physical kingdom but it is a system of authority that is found within the believer. *Now when He was asked by the Pharisees when the kingdom of God would come, He answered them and said, "The kingdom of God does not come with observation; nor will they say, 'See here!' or 'See there!' For indeed, the kingdom of God is within you"* (Luke 17:20-21). If we remove ourselves from the equation the Kingdom leaves with us.

The Kingdom requires partnership and agreement to function properly. The Father made all things for Himself but He desires to partner with us to display His glory in the earth. Nothing pleases Him more than when we choose to come into agreement with His heart by faith concerning anything and then allow His sovereignty to flow through us. We were created for intimacy to rule in the earth as He rules in the heavens.

Jesus demonstrated this truth over and over again as He moved throughout the earth releasing the Kingdom of Heaven. He stated that He could do nothing without first coming into agreement with the Father. *"I can of Myself do nothing. As I hear, I judge; and My judgment is righteous, because I do not seek My own will but the will of the Father who sent Me"* (John 5:30). I don't believe that Jesus was saying He was a robot receiving a command. He was saying that without partnering with His Father He would lack the ability to fulfill the Father's will. I believe He accomplished this as a man choosing to agree with the Father's invitation to partner with Him to release Heaven's goodness in the earth.

The Father has a desire to establish His will and His rule in the earth. Motivated by love He desires to partner with mankind in order to establish it. He uses all His available resources, those willing to partner with Him, in order to accomplish His will. He has created all things for Himself with a specific purpose, and at the appointed time He brings His creation into fullness. At that moment, His Kingdom of love and power awakens within us to destroy the works of the devil. The Father's Sovereign Government operates through partnership and agreement for these two purposes; to destroy the works of the devil and establish His rule in the earth.

The King of Kings

In America, we have a democratic government that is setup with an executive branch, a legislative branch and a judicial branch. Within our government the highest power is granted to the President. The President's responsibility is to "take care that the laws be faithfully executed," and to "preserve, protect, and defend the Constitution." In such a system no man can take this power but he must be given the power by election of the people. Therefore, his power is limited by the electing body through the process of impeachment.

Jesus, who is the King of the Kingdom of Heaven, did not take the authority and power given to Him. He was elected by the one who is the creator and source of all power in heaven and earth (see Mathew 3:17). He was not elected as a political leader by a constituency through a democratic vote. He was also not elected by a heavenly host or other form of power even though all has been put under Him. Unlike satan, whose authority is illegitimate and limited, Jesus was given all authority both in heaven and earth by the Father to rule His government.

As obvious as that may sound many fail to come to that conclusion. Many individuals and systems of authority such as churches, governments and corporations feel as if the Kingdom of God functions as a democracy. We as individuals do not have the authority to impeach Jesus or vote Him in or out. He was elected by the Father as the King and His election is irrevocable.

Jesus, having been elected by the Father, is set on his right hand as the sovereign King who possesses all power in heaven and earth. In fact, all things that were created were created by Him (John 1:3). Colossians 1:15-18 says, "*Who is the image of the invisible God, the firstborn of every creature: For by him were all things created, that are in heaven, and that are in earth, visible and invisible, whether they be thrones, or dominions, or principalities, or powers: all things were created by him, and for him: And he is before all things, and by him all things consist. And he is the head of the body, the church: who is the beginning, the firstborn from the dead; that in all things he might have the preeminence*". Jesus is the image of the invisible God being the firstborn of every creature. Nothing was made in Heaven or in the earth prior to Jesus or outside of His granted authority. Therefore He is perfect theology.

Jesus is Perfect Theology

The person of Jesus is perfect theology. All of our thoughts about God and His sovereignty must be filtered through the person of Jesus. All of our authority and power finds its source in Him. He is the head of the church and we must partner with Him to activate the Kingdom and bring its rule into the earth. Without Jesus we can do nothing. Outside of His rule we are helpless before the devil. When we align with His rule we find ourselves seated with Him in heavenly places high above all principalities and powers.

The devil was never a threat to Jesus even though He had emptied Himself of His authority and power (see Philippians 2:6-8). The gospels reveal to us that Holy Spirit descended up Him and remained after He was baptized in the Jordan River. As we discussed earlier, after this event He was taken by the Spirit into the wilderness to confront the devil.

Many view this confrontation in the wilderness as a struggle between good and evil. There was never a struggle nor will there ever be a struggle between Jesus and the devil. Holy Spirit was leading Him to His destiny; to take back the authority the devil had taken. Because He was victorious we are victorious in Him. The devil is not a threat to us either when we remain in Him.

For many the idea that the devil is not a threat to a Christian abiding in Christ is foreign. Many feel that because God allowed them to experience loss or trauma then He must have caused the circumstance to build character. Others feel He is punishing them for their sin or will quote Job's words that the Lord gives and takes away. These viewpoints contradict the Father's nature seen in the life of Jesus.

Jesus did not send a hurricane to bring judgment to a sinful city but rebuked the storm. He never made anyone sick but healed their sickness. He didn't stone the women caught in the act of adultery He granted her mercy. He didn't leave the lunatic filled with legions of demons to be tormented but cast out the devils and restored him to soundness of mind. He gave His life so we could walk in victory. The only thing Jesus took away from people was sickness, disease and all manner of oppression. Loss, sickness, disease and emotional distress are a reality in this world but let hope arise because He has overcome them all!

The Spirit of the Lord

I believe Jesus accomplished His victory over the devil, was able perform miracles and endure the cross by Holy Spirit working within Him and resting upon Him. By making this statement I am not saying that Jesus wasn't God when He walked the earth. I believe He was, is and will always be God. I am simply stating that as He partnered with the Father and came into agreement with His will, Holy Spirit brought His rule into the atmosphere.

The devil could do nothing to overcome Jesus in the wilderness because He came with the authority and the power of Holy Spirit. As Holy Spirit rested upon Him all that came to Him were healed, liberated and filled with the Father's goodness. It was Holy Spirit that gave Him the ability to overcome the grave and become a life giving spirit (see 1 Corinthians 15:45).

Holy Spirit rested upon Jesus and as a result Heaven invaded earth. Isaiah 11:2 says, *"The spirit of the Lord shall rest upon him; the spirit of wisdom and understanding, the spirit of counsel and might, the spirit of knowledge and the fear of the Lord. And shall make him of quick understanding in the fear of the LORD: and he shall not judge after the sight of his eyes, neither reprove after the hearing of his ears: But with righteousness shall he judge the poor, and reprove with equity for the meek of the earth: and he shall smite the earth with the rod of his mouth, and with the breath of his lips shall he slay the wicked"*.

Holy Spirit enabled Jesus to be righteous and walk in the fullness of the Father's glory. He came into this world as the Son of Man and ascended as the Son of God. As the Son of Man He demonstrated to us what was possible when Holy Spirit rests upon a willing vessel. Outside of Holy Spirit Jesus would not have been able to accomplish what He did. I can't really say that we need Holy Spirit more or less than He did. I just know we need Him desperately to live within us and rest upon us to bring Heavens rule into the earth.

There are many today who fail to see the importance of cultivating a relationship with God through His Spirit. Many shy away from His gifts in pursuit of His fruit being afraid of deception. I do agree that operating in the gifts without character is an illegal operation but the same is true in cultivating character without the gifts. The fruit of the Spirit and the gifts of the Spirit do not consistently function independently. They were both designed by God to bring His rule to the earth as they function together in unity.

Electing to stop the flow of the gifts of the Spirit is a very dangerous election regardless of the reasoning. The apostle Paul made this clear to us in his letter to the Thessalonians. *Quench not the Spirit* (1 Thessalonians 5:19). The Greek word for quench means to extinguish. I believe the implication here relates to not allowing a freedom of expression. Holy Spirit releases a diversity of gifts among the body to build us up and bring us into fullness. It is very hard for me to imagine that anyone would desire to extinguish the fire of Holy Spirit because of the many benefits His fire brings. But many do.

Electing to allow the flow of the gifts of the Spirit without cultivating the fruit of the Spirit is also a dangerous election regardless of the reasoning. The apostle Paul made this clear to us in his letter to the Ephesians. *And grieve not the Holy Spirit of God, whereby ye are sealed unto the day of redemption* (Ephesians 4:30). The Greek word for grieve here means to bring sorrow or to distress. I believe the implication here relates to embracing a lifestyle of sin or failing to allow Holy Spirit to transform us into the image of Christ. When the fruit of the Spirit is cultivated in our lives our soul prospers as our spirit enjoys communion with God. When we resurrect our sinful nature then we endure hardships we were never destined to endure.

Jesus was very adamant about the need for both the fruits evident in our character and the fruits evident in the signs and wonders that should follow us. We see this clearly when He gave His final instructions before ascending to His place at the right hand of the Father. He told them to go to Jerusalem and wait for the power that would come with the promised Spirit (see Acts 1:4-5). This baptism of fire would not only enable them to overcome their sinful nature but would also allow them to heal the sick, cast out devils, raise the dead and cleanse lepers.

Holy Spirit living within us cultivates righteous character. Righteousness is not attainable without the transforming power of Holy Spirit. Many have one form or another of self-righteousness that is based on their ability to maintain a set of values. Though I believe having the right values is important, true holiness is only produced by Holy Spirit dwelling in our hearts. All of our efforts to produce holiness by adhering to a set of rules will grieve Holy Spirit, lead to frustration and ultimately lead us away from God. Holy Spirit living within us produces the only holiness we will ever have.

Holy Spirit resting upon us produces the fruit of signs, wonders and miracles. We see this clearly portrayed in the life of Jesus. Prior to His baptism in the Jordan River when Holy Spirit descended upon Him and remained there is no record of Jesus performing miracles. Once he came out of the wilderness after overcoming the devil, all that came to Him were healed, delivered and filled with God's goodness.

Many point to the fast and the withstanding the temptation as the source of His power. I think those viewpoints have merit but I believe He went into the wilderness with the same power He came out with. It was Holy Spirit resting and remaining upon Him that allowed

Him to fast for forty days, withstand the temptation and take back the authority satan had stolen.

Holy Spirit is our connection to our King and our Father in Heaven. Without Him we are blind and unable to see the one whose image we are to take on. The promise Jesus spoke of to His disciples was that Holy Spirit living in us and resting upon us would enable us to be partakers of His nature (see 2 Peter 1:4). Holy Spirit enables us to see the reality of heaven. When we see heaven and choose to agree with its reality we are transformed from glory to glory. Heaven invades earth and we are able to rule as He rules.

Chapter 7

Activating the Kingdom

Mankind was crowned with honor and glory at the time of creation. The fall of Adam and Eve in the garden changed our state in this world. The ones whom God had chosen to establish His rule in the earth had found themselves being ruled by another spirit. When Jesus came everything changed. For the first time since the fall of mankind the, restoration was possible. The Kingdom was finally at hand.

We are created to rule in the earth as God rules in the heavens. His sovereign government flows through us as we align with His will and purposes. We have access to an ultimate partnership that enables us to rule with Him. Jesus has risen victorious and is now seated at the Father's right hand. By His blood we have access to reign with Him. He is the King and the church is His governing body. All fullness dwells in Him and by Holy Spirit all fullness dwells in us corporately.

The Church, *ekklesia* in Greek, is His governing body empowered by Holy Spirit to establish heavens rule. When Jesus walked the earth the term *ekklesia* was used by the Romans to describe a group of individuals given the charge to transform the culture of a conquered territory. When Simon Peter made his declaration that Jesus was the Christ, Jesus made His declaration of His plans to transform the earth. *Now I say to you that you are Peter, and upon this rock I will build my church and the gates of hell will not prevail against it* (Matthew 16:18).

Jesus then said something that would take generations to unfold. *And I will give you the keys of the Kingdom of Heaven. Whatever you forbid on the earth will be forbidden in heaven, and whatever you permit on earth will be permitted in heaven* (Matthew 16:19). There are keys of the Kingdom of Heaven and they give His church, *ekklesia*, the authority to legislate what is permitted and what is not permitted. For some this may sound foreign but at our core we were created to rule as He rules. Jesus is alive within us to bring heavens rule to every facet of our lives and cultures.

The Just Shall Live by Faith

Faith is the core principle that allows us to move in such authority. For many, faith is an abstract concept that lacks true dimension but the opposite is true. Faith is a very tangible concrete principle that has measureable dimensions. We begin with a measure of faith and then we move from one level to the next (see Romans 12:3; 2 Corinthians 10:15).

Jesus had much to say about faith. It seemed to be His main concern with respect to His disciples. There are four occasions in the Gospel of Matthew that He uses the phrase, *"O ye of little faith"*. When teaching a parable of an unjust judge He says, *"when the Son of man comes will He find faith on the earth?"* (see Luke 18:8). When answering a man whose son was not healed when His disciples prayed for him He explained that is was because of a lack of faith (see Matthew 17:20).

The subject of faith was also a main theme of the apostle Paul in his letters to the churches. On four occasions he quotes a verse found in Habakkuk 2 which says, "*the just shall live by faith*". The Hebrew here is *tsaddiyq chayah emuwnah,* which is more perfectly translated as "the righteous one is revived and continues to be revived by his faithfulness". It is our faithfulness to our divine purpose that enables us to sustain life. As we find the Lord trustworthy and He finds us trustworthy then abundant life dominates our existence.

True Righteousness Produces Heavens Justice

True righteousness produces Heavens justice in the earth. I believe this is one of the keys that Jesus was speaking of in Matthew 16:19. Righteousness is the ability to judge correctly between good and evil. Once evil has been identified then good must be legislated.

Many view righteousness from a works oriented foundation thinking that it is godly behavior. Godly behavior is a fruit of righteousness but falls short of its true purpose. Righteousness finds its beginning in the power of the blood of Jesus to purge our conscience of dead works. Once Holy Spirit's dwelling place has been prepared by the blood of Jesus then He inhabits. Only then do we fully demonstrate righteousness.

This truth is illustrated to us when Jesus approaches John the Baptist in the wilderness and requests to be baptized. The reason for His request was to fulfill all righteousness. Jesus was without sin so this baptism wasn't to cleanse Him of sin but to prepare Him to receive Holy Spirit. After Jesus comes out of the water the heavens open and Holy Spirit descends upon Him like a dove and remained (see Matthew 3:16).

All righteousness could not be fulfilled until Holy Spirit rested upon Jesus and remained. The purpose of righteousness is revealed when He is taken by the Spirit in the wilderness to confront the devil. Holy Spirit resting on our lives enables us to do what Jesus did; destroy the works of the devil. True righteousness produces heavens justice in the earth by destroying the works of the devil.

Faith Defined

Faith is much more than just our ability to believe. The gift of faith granted to us produces righteousness within us. The righteousness produced by the blood of Jesus enables us to receive Holy Spirit by faith. The reviving life He brings to us is sustained as we move from one level of faith to the next.

The writer of Hebrews defined faith as the substance of things hoped for and the evidence of the unseen (see Hebrews 11:1). I see this definition as our ability to see Christ, the hope of glory, and trust Him to transform us into His image. By adding this definition to the verse in Habakkuk 2 we see a fuller picture of the just living by faith; the righteous one is revived and continues to be revived by his ability to see Christ the hope of glory and trust Him to transform us into His image.

Jesus, the righteous one, demonstrated this truth to us so masterfully. He was not moved or motivated by obstacles, storms, sickness, disease or even death. He taught us that all things are possible to those who believe and then demonstrated this truth over and over again. He was motivated by what He heard the Father saying and what He saw the Father doing. He came in the image of the Father revealing His heart to the world. He then said we can do the same and more (see John 14:12).

Activating the Kingdom

We are the body of Christ and possess all His fullness. As such, we also have the invitation to live in the miraculous realm of the Kingdom by faith. Jesus is the head of His body revealing to us the Father's heart. As we abide in Him and He in us there is a transfer of His kingship upon our lives. Our appetite for the unseen world of Heaven invading earth should be fueled by knowing we are sons and daughters of God and joint heirs with Christ. We are the Father's chosen vessels consecrated to represent Him until Jesus comes to join us to bring total victory.

The apostle Paul revealed this truth to the church in Corinth in his writings to them. *Nevertheless when one turns to the Lord, the veil is taken away. Now the Lord is that Spirit; and where the Spirit of the Lord is there is liberty. But we all, with open face beholding as in a mirror the glory of the Lord, are changed into the same image from glory to glory, even as by the Spirit of the Lord* (2 Corinthians 3:16-18). By faith we are able to see the Father of glory. As we trust Him we are transformed into His image of glory by Holy Spirit. Faith sees the Fathers glory and hope hungers for His glory to invade the earth until it manifests.

If Jesus did all that He did as God I am extremely impressed but He walked the earth as a man. Here again I am not saying that Jesus is not God; He is and will always be. He emptied Himself of all His divine power and authority when He descended to the earth (see Philippians 2:7). He was conceived by Holy Spirit to become the seed of the woman. He walked the earth as the Son of Man and the Son of God. Holy Spirit lived within Him enabling Him to fulfill the Law. Holy Spirit rested upon Him enabling Him to perform miracles. Holy Spirit transformed Him into the image of the Fathers glory.

Holy Spirit activated the Kingdom of Heaven in Jesus. The Son of Man, born of a woman, was transformed into the Son of God to destroy the works of the devil. Through His blood we are given the right to do the same. His blood purges our conscience of dead works. His word washes over us and liberates us from deception. His baptism revives our spirit and enables us to do greater works than He did. Through the veil of His body we have access to heavens resources. By faith in Him the Kingdom of Heaven within us is activated and grows until it prevails.

The Kingdom of Heaven cannot be activated in our lives through spiritual disciplines alone. All we do to discipline ourselves spiritually should be leading us to an encounter with Holy Spirit. Our gatherings should bring people to the place of encounter. Our devotion time should be more than an intellectual exercise to understand principles and concepts. Our bible is filled with powerful life giving truth but its liberating power is not fully activated until we encounter the one who is the word become flesh. We must gain experiential knowledge of the realm where we are seated; with Christ in heavenly places.

Prayer is a powerful thing when it is done as Jesus taught; declaring the earth to look like heaven. Many approach prayer in a very systematic way using a focus or a list. Focusing on needs and directives is an effective form of prayer but it lacks power if it's not in harmony with heavens orchestra. As I have grown into this understanding I find myself leaving my prayer list behind and just communing with the Lord. This has totally revolutionized the effectiveness of my prayer time.

I have come to the conclusion that my only discipline should be cultivating a relationship with Holy Spirit. He is the one Jesus has sent to lead me, empower me, comfort me and strengthen me. He activates the kingdom within me. As I read my bible I wait to encounter Him and then feed on the bread He has led me to. As I pray He strengthens me and reveals the Father's heart enabling me to command earth to take on heavens form. As I fast I wait for Him to lead me to the devil and then overcome him as Jesus did. As I commune with Him I am filled with power to do what I was created to do; destroy the works of the devil and establish God's rule in the earth.

Chapter 8

Releasing the Kingdom

The testimony of Jesus's life found in the gospels is always so amazing to me. At His baptism Heaven opened and Holy Spirit descended upon Him and remained. From that day forward nothing would be the same for Him or the world around Him. He demonstrated to us a reality that seems impossible to attain. The really amazing thing is that He informed us that we have access to this reality and more.

When I study American church cultures functioning today I come to some very interesting conclusions. It seems that somewhere along the way we lost focus of the main thing; bringing Heavens reality into earth. Most traditional church's today place a high regard on humanism, intellectualism and humanitarian efforts. I certainly don't have an issue with improving our quality of life, gaining knowledge through education or helping others in need. All of these are needed but releasing God's Kingdom by creating a place for Holy Spirit to rest should be primary.

Thousands flock to events focused on raising money for some form of medical research or social reform. When a natural disaster happens organizations join forces to send resources in the form of supplies or people to help. These are good things but they are reactionary in nature. The Kingdom is not reactionary but is proactive through partnership and agreement. Most spend their time focusing on problems rather than focusing on the one who has the solution; Holy Spirit.

Jesus was focused on one thing; the heart of the Father. It was from that foundation that heaven flowed through Him. He was so connected to the Father that He remained in His perfect will. We do not find a single account of Jesus seeking an answer through prayer when confronted with a problem. He already spent time communing with the Father so He had the answer living within Him and resting upon Him. He declared healing and it happened. He commanded the storm to be still and it was. Every ounce of His strength was put towards bringing heavens reality in earth.

Somewhere along the way we limited the Kingdom of God to increasing human strength through numbers and focus on education. Sunday mornings are focused on the sermon rather than His presence. The salvation message has been reduced to our eternal resting place rather than living as a new creation. Evangelism has been diminished to inviting people to church. Most that is done to focus on and advance the Kingdom lacks faith and in turn lacks the realm of the miraculous.

Discerning Spiritual Atmospheres

Jesus's message to humanity was and is, *"Repent for the Kingdom is at hand"*. As I mentioned earlier this simply means to change the way we think. When our mind is transformed and renewed to see Heavens reality then all of Heaven's resources become available to us. Releasing the Kingdom in the earth is very simply identifying Heavens reality and then bringing that reality into the earth by faith.

Jesus rebuked both leading religious groups among the Jews at the time He walked the earth. He called them hypocrites because they were unable to discern the spiritual atmosphere of their day. *When it is evening, you say, "it will be fair weather because the sky is red". And in the morning you say, "it will be foul weather today because the sky is red and lowring". You hypocrites, you can discern the face of the sky; but can you not discern the signs of the times?* (Matthew 16:1-3 ASV) Even though they had seen all the signs, wonders and miracles Jesus had performed, up to this point they still could not discern Heaven's reality standing before them.

Our ability to discern what is available or what aspect of the Kingdom is at hand is vital to releasing it. We have no record of the woman with the issue of blood receiving teaching on receiving healing by touching the hem of Jesus's garment. In spite of this, somehow she was able to discern that it was available to her. There were many others in the crowd that touched Jesus but she was the only one who accessed healing. Some may argue there may have been others who were touched as well but the scripture doesn't reveal them. The implication is she discerned something others did not.

The man at the pool of Bethesda was only aware healing was available when the water stirred until Jesus informed him of another reality. Jesus's first miracle of turning water into wine seemed to happen before it was time but somehow His mother discerned it was available. The Canaanite women whom Jesus referred to as a dog also received the children's bread before it was time for the gospel to be released to the Gentiles. Even after Jesus informed her He had come to the lost sheep of Israel she was able to look into Heaven's reality and pull it into her situation.

There is some part of our person that is aware of God's presence when we find ourselves in it. When the Spirit begins to move in a service people react differently. Some shake, some laugh, some cry, some shout, some run, some kneel or lie down, some have inspired thought and others feel overwhelming peace. The list goes on and on. The point is our physical body and emotions react to God's presence. The difficult part at times is recognizing our physical or emotional reaction as God's presence, especially when He is teaching us to recognize Him in new ways.

The writer of Hebrews revealed to us that those who are mature are able to discern good and evil by exercising their senses. *For everyone that uses milk is unskillful in the word of righteousness: for he is a babe. But strong meat belongs to them that are of full age, even those who by reason of use have their senses exercised to discern both good and evil* (Hebrews 5:14 KJV). The more time we spend in God's presence the more we are able to discern Him with all our senses. As Holy Spirit lives within us and rests upon us, all of our senses are enhanced enabling us to see, feel, smell, taste and hear the difference between Heaven's reality and any other reality.

During the process of flight training pilots are instructed to learn how their body reacts to a low oxygen environment. They are placed in a flight simulator with a pad and pen and the instructors begin to reduce the oxygen levels. They then tell the pilot to write down any feelings they are experiencing. Some may feel pain in their shoulder others may begin to feel dizzy. The point of the exercise is to get the pilot to know when the oxygen levels in the plane have diminished to a dangerous level so he can react if the sensors fail. If the oxygen sensors fail and the pilot fails to recognize a drop in oxygen in the plane then all the passengers die.

The Sadducees and Pharisees thought they had the ability to discern right judgment because they had the Law and their Traditions. The issue was their eyes had been blinded and their ears had been deafened because they chose a reality that lacked God's presence. For generations they had allowed their senses to be trained by a lower reality. When Jesus, the one who is Heavens reality, was among them they couldn't discern Him. Traditions dull the senses and nullify the authoritative prescription of Heaven's reality. Recognizing what is available to us, even when we it goes against our traditional beliefs, brings abundant life into every situation.

Power and Authority

Our ability to properly and consistently bring Heavens reality into the earth depends upon many things. Once we discern what is available we have to understand how the power and authority of Heaven flows through us to change the conditions around us. There has been much teaching throughout history about releasing the Kingdom through power and authority. Some groups emphasize authority or our covenant rights as believers neglecting power. Others put a greater emphasis on power or our ability to move in signs, wonders and miracles neglecting authority. This is an illegal divorce. Power and Authority must be exercised together in order to truly prevail against the gates of hell.

There are a couple of Greek words used in the New Testament that are translated as power. The one most relating to the flow of signs wonders and miracles is *dynamis* and the one relating to authority is *exousia*. Exousia relates to our rights as believers, mainly our right to rule. In his epistle to the Romans, Paul informed them that the Gospel of Christ is the authority of God that brings salvation. This gospel also reveals God's righteousness and enables us to move from one level of faith to another (see Romans 1:16-17).

The apostle John gives a similar but yet different viewpoint. *But as many as received Him, to them He gave the authority to become the sons of God, even them that believe in His name; Which were born, not of blood, nor of the will of the flesh, nor of the will of man, but of God* (John 1:12-13). When we receive Christ we are granted the authority to be born of God. Our salvation experience elevates us beyond our blood line, our fallen nature and our own desires. Through Christ we are adopted by the Father of the universe and become heirs to His throne.

There are many who fail to access all the benefits of our adoption. Some feel as if they cannot be used by God to release His Kingdom because they don't come from a long of line of ministers. Others feel their sinful past has disqualified them. There is another group who feel they lack the education but our adoption as children of God supersedes all of these. We are qualified through Christ to access Heaven's resources not our family history, life experience or education.

Authority is Our Birthright

Authority is our birthright when we are born into God's Kingdom. The level of authority we are granted depends greatly on our level of faithfulness to live a life in His presence. This truth is revealed to us in the garden when Adam and Eve failed to rule their environment as God had instructed. They failed to faithfully fulfill their obligations by eating the fruit from the tree they were forbidden and hiding from God's presence. Because of their unfaithfulness mankind would have to go through the process of building God's trust again before their authority was fully restored.

The life of Abraham illustrates this truth as well. As Abram continued to walk with God in relationship he became the one who would carry the fullness of God's promise to restore mankind in seed form. God's promise to him was that through him all the nations of the earth would be blessed. Through Abraham all nations would have the opportunity to be restored back to their original glory. They would be given access to Heaven's resources to rule in the earth as God rules.

There was an instance in Abrahams life that reveals to us the level of authority he was granted. God looked upon the cities of Sodom and Gomorrah and decided that He was going to destroy them because of their wickedness. Rather than release His judgment He talks with Abraham about it first. I believe this was a test to see if Abraham could handle the level of authority he was going to be granted. God wanted to see how much of His nature had been imparted to Abraham while they communed together.

Rather than agreeing with God that these cities deserved to be destroyed, Abraham begins to intercede for them. Having mercy and compassion for those who are under the power of sin is one way we are granted more authority. God chooses to save Lot and his family because Abraham chose to intercede for them.

I wonder how many natural disasters would be averted if we as the body of Christ were moved by mercy and compassion to intercede for cities that are captured by the power of sin. I also wonder how much more authority the church of America would have to transform our nation if we were to change our thinking in regards to the areas plagued by sin. Authority is our birthright to rule the way God rules.

Our Ability to Rule

Authority is our right to rule but power gives us the ability to rule effectively. Jesus's disciples walked with Him for three years watching Him demonstrate how to release the Kingdom. Because they were under His influence their lives had already began to change. One might think that they would be able to fulfill all Jesus commanded just because they were with Him but that wasn't the case. Jesus had one final commandment before He ascended into heaven; wait in Jerusalem until you receive power (see Acts 1:8).

Jesus's command to wait for power has always fascinated me. They had already performed miracles when they were commissioned with seventy others to heal the sick (see Luke 10:17). Obviously the level of power released to them earlier wasn't sufficient to release the Kingdom in the way Jesus intended after His ascension. They needed something more than the authority they had already received. They needed Holy Spirit to rest upon them like He rested upon Jesus.

The disciples lived under Jesus's anointing umbrella while He was with them prior to His ascension but He gave them the same anointing He had once He ascended. It is totally acceptable to depend on someone else's anointing for a season but there comes a time when we need to have our own anointing. There are seasons in our life where we are able to ride the wave of yesterday's victory but there comes a time when we need more. There comes a day when we can no longer access the level of power we need the way we did in the past.

The disciples along with the seventy others had been demonstrating power under the shadow of what Jesus carried but He wasn't always going to be with them. The idea of Jesus leaving was quite troubling to the disciples but He told them to rejoice. Once He returned to the Father, Holy Spirit would be released to teach them all things and allow them to remember what they had learned. The power that was coming to Jerusalem to rest upon them would take them into dimensions they could not experience while He was with them.

After Holy Spirit was poured upon those in the upper room on the day of Pentecost it seems Jesus's disciples understood why it had to be that way. Authority without the continual power to exercise it is quite useless. Many have a form of godliness but lack the power to demonstrate what they believe. This almost always leads to a diminished weak and feeble gospel that lacks the ability to change the world. The Gospel of Christ is filled life changing power that heals the body, liberates the soul and revives the Spirit.

Jesus's ability to demonstrate the power of the Kingdom was the thing that authenticated His identity. *Then came the Jews round about Him, and said, "How long will you make us to doubt? If you are the Christ, tell us plainly". Jesus answered them, "I told you, and you did not believe: the works that I do in my Father's name, they bear witness of me"* (John 10:24-25). The same would be true of the disciples after they received power from Holy Spirit resting upon them (see Acts 1:8). Holy Spirit resting upon us enables us to do works in Jesus's name that bear witness to our identity in Him as we do what He did and more.

Working with Holy Spirit

Jesus's message was undeniably clear. He came to destroy the works of the devil and reconcile mankind to the Father. He multiplied bread and fish by giving thanks. He healed a blind man by spitting in mud and rubbing it in his eyes. He resurrected Lazarus with a three word declaration. A woman was healed by touching the hem of His garment. Lepers were healed as they walked to present themselves at the temple for evaluation. As we read of Jesus's miracles there is only one common theme; He stayed connected to the Father through Holy Spirit to release His will in the earth (see John 5:30).

I have found in my pursuit of signs, wonders and miracles that I don't always have clear instructions as to how to release heaven. Methods change often and rapidly at times and should not be our focus. Rather than focusing on methods I have purposed in my heart to learn how to work alongside Holy Spirit. He can use whatever available resources He has to release the miraculous in any situation. If I present to someone a method that may have worked in the past I have no guarantee of results. If is present the person of Holy Spirit I know something will happen.

Earlier I mentioned the importance of discerning spiritual atmospheres. When seeking the Lord for discernment it is important that we seek what Holy Spirit desires and then come into alignment with it. Many seek to understand the demonic realm and pray to discern which demon is at work. Not being ignorant of the devils devises is a good thing but over emphasizing them is dangerous work. If we catch a glimpse of the Fathers heart and align with Holy Spirit to release it in the earth all of hells demons lack the power to stop it, whether we know which one is at work or not.

Discerning what Holy Spirit desires can be rather difficult at times but it must be our focus. Intentionally or unintentionally using a method that Holy Spirit is not requiring of us quenches His work in our lives. Some may feel this is harsh and non-relational but Holy Spirit is not a harsh dictator. He carries the heart of the Father and when we align with Him through obedience power flows through us.

King Saul was given specific instructions concerning the Amalekites after he had been anointed king. Prior to this the prophet Samuel had given him instructions to go to the hill of God where Holy Spirit would come upon him transforming him into a new man (see 1 Samuel 10:6). I believe this was a preview of what was going to be released through Jesus; Holy Spirit coming upon men to transform them into the image of Christ.

Saul got it right the first time and began to prophecy, an ability he did not possess prior this occasion. He then failed to follow the instructions given to him to destroy the Amalekites and Holy Spirit departed. He chose his own way and suffered the worst punishment imaginable; a life void of Holy Spirit. Had he repented when Samuel confronted him I believe his end would have been much more glorious. When we fail there is always a plan of redemption to get us back on track if we are willing to humble ourselves and change our thinking.

Working with the Angels

Some fourteen years after Jesus ascended the power and authority He released to His disciples was producing great fruit. The Gospel of the Kingdom had made its way outside of Jerusalem and was affecting most parts of the Roman Empire. About the time that many apostles and prophets left Jerusalem to meet in Antioch, James the brother of John was arrested by Herod the king (see Acts 12:1).

The events that transpired after James was arrested are quite interesting to say the least. Herod proceeds to murder James. The reaction by the Jews is quite appalling as they were quite pleased with the death of one of their kinsman. When Herod saw their reaction he then arrested Peter and sought to do the same in an attempt to gain more favor with the Jews. When Peter was arrested he was placed in a prison with sixteen Roman soldiers guarding him.

Once the other leaders and disciples heard what had happened they prayed without ceasing. *Peter therefore was kept in prison: but prayer was made without ceasing of the church unto God for him* (Acts 12:5). On the night before he was set to executed Peter was sleeping in his shackles and all of the sudden an angel of the Lord struck him waking him up. The angel told him to get up and follow him out of the prison. Peter wasn't sure if what was happening was real or not as he was following the angel.

This historical account of Peter being liberated from prison is a powerful testimony of how angels are sent when we pray without ceasing. My point here isn't that we must continue in prayer, although I believe Peter's testimony illustrates that as well. My point is that we have access to heavens army who help us accomplish our assignments here in the earth. There is a multitude of angels who are given instructions from our Father to assist us as we partner with Him.

Another testimony in the scripture that illustrates this truth is found during the reign of King Jehoshaphat. *And when he had consulted with the people, he appointed singers unto the LORD, and that should praise the beauty of holiness, as they went out before the army, and to say, "Praise the LORD; for his mercy endureth forever". And when they began to sing and to praise, the LORD set ambushments against the children of Ammon, Moab, and mount Seir, which were come against Judah; and they were smitten* (2 Chronicles 20:21-22). These ambushments were heavens army assisting God's people to win a battle they could not win alone.

The angels of the Lord are ministering spirits sent to minister to those who are to be heirs of salvation. They are sent with one mission; to ensure the Father's will is accomplished in the earth. As we align with Holy Spirit concerning the Father's heart we release His manifold wisdom to the angelic host which enables them to publish His word (see Ephesians 3:10).

Many reject teaching about angels and the importance they have because of distorted viewpoints about how they function. The scriptures are very clear that they are sent to minister to us and assist us. Rejecting this truth limits our effectiveness to bring Heaven's rule into the earth because the angels are a part of Heaven's Government. I believe that rejecting their assistance is one of the ways Holy Spirit becomes grieved and eventually departs from us.

Taking Risk

When we examine the life of Jesus there are many things we see working within Him. One thing that we don't see is fear. He knew the suffering He would have to endure becoming the sacrificial Lamb of God. Yet He approached the cross without fear. His life was in danger many times before He laid it down but that did not deter Him. He seemed to have an unrelenting ability to take risk in order to see the Father's will established.

Jesus would heal on the Sabbath day in the Synagogue knowing that some, if not all in attendance, would not view this favorably. He spoke to those that most would not. He touched lepers without fear of being infected. He ran those out of the Temple who were selling items of sacrifice knowing it would cause uproar among the leaders. Over and over again He risked His life and reputation releasing the Kingdom everywhere He went.

The way Jesus reflected and relayed this value of risk taking to His disciples was quite profound. *These twelve Jesus sent out, instructing them, "Go nowhere among the Gentiles and enter no town of the Samaritans, but go rather to the lost sheep of the house of Israel. And proclaim as you go, saying, 'The kingdom of heaven is at hand.' Heal the sick, raise the dead, cleanse lepers, cast out demons. You received without paying; give without pay. Acquire no gold or silver or copper for your belts, no bag for your journey, or two tunics or sandals or a staff, for the laborer deserves his food"* (Matthew 10:5-10).

Jesus didn't send them to a school to learn how to heal the sick. He just commanded them to do it. They hadn't attended Resurrecting 101 or attended a conference on how to cast out devils. The only education they had received was watching Jesus take risk as they walked with Him. I definitely don't have a problem with education or conferences that equip us to do the work of the ministry but I do have a problem with not taking action.

Jesus instructed His disciples to go empty handed. They were not instructed to send out sponsorship letters, visit local church's or stand on street corners trying to raise money. They couldn't even bring an extra set of cloths when they went. After they ministered they couldn't take up an offering or receive an honorarium. As they labored declaring the Kingdom of Heaven provisions would be made. I have to say that when I read these verses Jesus's form of leadership is uncomfortable for me.

As a leader I feel obligated to ensure those under my direction are protected and provided for but Jesus approached this specific assignment differently. He was creating an environment that would require His disciples to take risk in order to fulfill His requests. They were sent out not with methods of how to accomplish what they were being asked to do but with simple directives that came with Heaven's authority. The authority that Jesus conveyed to them as He made His request was provision enough for them to accomplish all they were asked to do.

The amount of trust Jesus exercised by granting His disciples such authority without formal training is quite profound. He knew that they would make mistakes and fail often but He was willing to allow them to take risk without fear of being rejected by Him. He was willing to risk His own reputation so they could grow in confidence in the message He was conveying. There are probably many more reasons why He did this but one is very evident to me; a gospel without risk is not the Gospel of the Kingdom of Heaven.

Finding the Place to Rest Your Peace

Peace, more specifically world peace, seems to be a major subject among world groups no matter what their affiliation. There seems to be a longing in the heart of every individual to have world peace. Contestants of beauty pageants mention it as one of their life goals. Government groups seek to strategize to make it a reality. Groups host large rallies and concerts pledging to devote their efforts towards it. However, most if not all fail to recognize that peace is not a way of life but a person and true peace is not without conflict.

One of the movements that I believe propelled our nation into a state of lawlessness had a false reality of peace at its center. Woodstock, whose slogan was Three Days of Peace, was a concert designed to protest the Vietnam War in 1969. These so-called three days of peace were filled with drunkenness, drug abuse and fornication. It was from this foundation of celebrating peace that the powers of darkness shifted a nation away from the things of God. The subject of peace has powerful influence and many distort it to push their agendas.

One of the names given to Jesus by the prophet Isaiah is the Prince of Peace. Jesus in the person of peace that all mankind longs for. Releasing Him into a situation should be the focus of all ministry time. Much that we call ministry today lacks the unseen dimension of heaven where the Prince of Peace resides. If we are not living and ministering the Kingdom of Heaven from the dimension of heaven then what we are doing is not pleasing to God; without faith it is impossible to please Him.

As Jesus trained His disciples in Ministry 101 releasing His peace was a major theme. "*And whatever town or village you enter, find out who is worthy in it and stay there until you depart. And when you go into a household greet it. If the household is worthy, let your peace come upon it. But if it is not worthy, let your peace return to you. And whoever will not receive you nor hear your words, when you depart from that house or city, shake off the dust from your feet. Assuredly I say to you it will be more tolerable for the land of Sodom and Gomorrah in the day of judgment than for that city!'* The level of trust and authority displayed here is astonishing. Peace was to be released to those who received the message of the Kingdom and remain. It was withdrawn from those who rejected it.

The responsibility conveyed in Jesus's words is quite sobering to me. The atmosphere of heaven was released to everyone but not everyone received it. There were no instructions to release blessing only peace. One of the implications here is that true peace brings Heaven's resources with it; fullness of blessing. There were also no instructions here to express mercy in the sense of releasing peace to those who were unworthy. This message is highly unpopular in both our secular and church culture here in America. Both are filled with individuals who feel a sense of entitlement to receive things whether they deserve it or not.

True peace is not without conflict. *And the God of peace will crush satan under your feet shortly* (Romans 16:20). Paul's choice of words to the Romans seems rather contradictory. One might expect him to reference the Lord of Hosts rather the God of peace. When the Prince of Peace is released into an atmosphere those ready to receive Him rejoice but those influenced by the powers of darkness react much differently. The same person who fulfills the universal desire of all mankind destroys the works of the devil in the same expression.

True biblical peace is not a world without war or a euphoric state of harmony. It is the restoration of mankind that enables him to gain divine perspective and bear the image of Christ. When peace, which is divine perspective, is released into a hospital room sickness has to bow. When it is released into a domestic dispute or a counseling session the powers of darkness have to flee. Bringing God's perspective into any situation releases Heaven's reality and gives all involved the opportunity to receive victory.

Heavens Resources

The Father's Government has unlimited resources. We have an all-powerful all-knowing Father who is able to create a way where there is no way. There is no sickness more powerful than the blood of Jesus. There is no circumstance that causes God to say, "Sorry I can't help you with that one". As we draw close to Him this reality becomes more and more apparent.

A child's viewpoint on resources is quite amazing to me. They have no problem asking for things they want. They ask with a strong conviction their desire will be fulfilled. At times the conviction is so strong they demonstrate to the world their disappointment when they are informed they can't have what they want. Most call this a temper tantrum. They don't realize there are limitations until they are informed there are limitations.

We live in a finite world but as Christians our reality is an infinite reality. As embarrassing as it is when our child stomps and shouts in public when they don't get what they want they are operating in a superior reality. Their failure to control their emotions is not what I am speaking of. I am speaking of their conviction of the reality with unlimited resources to provide for their needs and desires.

Earlier we discussed the way Jesus sent out His disciples to release the Kingdom. He told them to heal sick, cleanse lepers, raise the dead and cast out devils without any apparent instructions or provisions. I believe He was giving them an opportunity to experience provision Heavens way. They were being trained how to walk with Holy Spirit. Jesus had enabled them to live under the umbrella of the Father's goodness with Holy Spirit for a season. He was training them not to seek after natural things but to long for Heaven's resources to invade their lives as they walked with Holy Spirit after His ascension.

I have found that many times I want God to supply me with all the natural resources up front I feel are needed to accomplish His will for my life before I can move forward. It takes resources to build and advance the Kingdom of God but we often forget the seed principle of the Kingdom. It is a good thing to count the cost before we give ourselves over to something but the cost should not limit us to start with what we have. When needing to feed over five thousand people Jesus took what was available to Him at the moment and multiplied it to supply the need. Holy Spirit alive within us and resting upon us is provision enough to ensure we have what we need in the moment.

Many say faith is Heaven's currency that allows us access Heaven's resources. I agree as long as faith is our ability to see our Father's glory and trust Holy Spirit to transform us so we bear the same image of glory. Our

Father is healing. He is provision, peace, holiness and so much more. When we take on His nature all of His resources become available to us to do what we were destined to do; destroy the works of the devil and establish the Fathers rule in the earth.

The Fathers Desire

Jesus came to accomplish many things. He came to fulfill the law, bring a sword of division, to seek and to save that which was lost and many other things. I agree with the apostle John that His primary purpose was to destroy the works of the devil (see 1 John 3:8). This however wasn't accomplished by using a set of religious exercises or a list of rules. He accomplished this by revealing the Father's heart.

Jesus came in the image of the Father to destroy the works of devil. Earlier we learned Adam and Eve had embraced one another with a lower reality and hid themselves from the Father in the garden. This transgression sent all mankind into a tail spin of death and destruction until his heart was only wicked. Grieved in heart God chose to eliminate this wicked generation using a flood even though His first nature is not judgment (see Genesis 6:5-7).

Some feel that when the Kingdom is released it brings judgment to the sinner. This viewpoint is however not the Fathers heart. He desires that not one person should perish under the power of sin. Jesus's message to the sinner was not a message of judgment by a message of freedom and hope. Those who chose to reject Him and embrace their traditions were the ones who received the message of judgment.

The miracles, signs and wonders displayed as Jesus destroyed the works of the devil were not designed to be the primary focus. This may seem contradictory because Jesus often pointed to His works to reveal His identity. The real focus of Jesus's life was to reveal to mankind that a life intertwined with the Father produces life. The miracles, signs and wonders were the fruit of a life fully committed to the Father.

Our Father desires our heart. He desires to be with us. Miracles are as easy as breathing for Him. It is from the foundation of relationship that He desires to allow that same power to flow through us. Releasing the Kingdom is not performance based even though it takes a method to release it. The method we use isn't the focus; the King who delegates authority and Holy Spirit who empowers us is.

As we gaze into our Father's eyes supernatural ability is released that enables us to live in total victory. Communing with Him face to face brings our identity to fruition. Noah, who was saved from the flood, found grace in the eyes of God. He wasn't saved by his education or his pedigree. His physical stature didn't qualify him to build the ark. He chose to commune with the Father face to face which qualified him for freedom from judgment.

As we pursue a life destroying the works of the devil we must keep the Father's desire our desire. He desires to be with us. We are the object of His love not an army of robots programmed to perform a task. He desires to pour His love upon us. When we choose to pour our love on Him then we are qualified and empowered to release His Kingdom on a consistent basis. This is important to mention because any other focus will eventually lead us away from His goodness and His resources.

Abiding in Him

Heaven is only filled with things that are good according to God's definition of goodness. Sickness or disease cannot be found in biblical descriptions of Heaven. What we do see is a place filled with perfect order and abundance. The Father's brilliance and radiance invades every part of it eliminating darkness. There is no question of His goodness or His sovereignty.

Many are unsure about who God is and how He operates. He does not release sickness and disease or death and destruction in the earth. Earlier I stated that the person of Jesus is perfect theology and we must gain our image of the Father from Him. If we fail to see God as He is then we lack the desire to abide in Him. Who wants to be in relationship with a God who lacks mercy and is constantly bringing harsh correction? He does bring correction but it comes through love that preserves and empowers not judgment that destroys and disables.

At times it is quite overwhelming to me to think my assignment is to bring Heaven into earth. When I become overwhelmed most times I will step back and redefine my focus. Focus is a very powerful principle that always enables me to keep the main thing the main thing.

My assignment is to destroy the works of the devil and establish my Father's order in the earth but my focus must be the one who loves me.

The turnover rate among preachers in America is quite staggering. Many start full of zeal and desirous to do good works but end up walking away for a number of reasons; both good and bad. I believe one main cause of this is our failure as leaders to properly equip individuals to do the work of the ministry. It is the responsibility of leadership to create a safe environment, a garden, filled with God's presence where people can grow into maturity.

Our ability to bring Heaven into the earth is not produced through our own faculties. Education is not the answer but a single tool that fits into our tool kit. We must stay connected to the one who enables us to access Heaven's resources; Holy Spirit. Our relationship with Him is crucial to enable us to stand firm until we consistently see Heaven invade earth.

At the Passover Celebration before the crucifixion Jesus begins to inform His disciples that He will soon be leaving them. This was quite troubling to them but Jesus told them not be troubled. In the middle of what appeared to be His final instructions, He reveals to them they would not be alone. *If ye love me, keep my commandments. And I will pray the Father, and he shall give you another Comforter, that he may abide with you for ever; Even the Spirit of truth; whom the world cannot receive, because it seeth him not, neither knoweth him: but ye know him; for he dwelleth with you, and shall be in you* (John 14:15-17).

Jesus begins to turn His disciples focus away from Him in the sense that He was informing them of the one who would take them into the fullness of what He introduced to them. *These things have I spoken unto you, being present with you. But the Comforter, Holy Spirit, whom the Father will send in my name, he shall teach you all things, and bring all things to your remembrance, whatsoever I have said unto you* (John 14:25-26). Many fail to realize that the way we fulfill Jesus's commandment to abide in Him is actually accomplished by abiding in Holy Spirit. Holy Spirit is our connection to the one who pours His goodness upon us and through us.

There is much effort given by many who are attempting to obey the sayings of Jesus without the assistance of Holy Spirit. Most times this leads to an outward form of holiness or godliness with a lack of power. Many fail to experience God's goodness because the God they know only looks to discipline them with rules and regulations. Others fail because of a misconception that holiness is not required. God demands holiness; just not the kind we can produce void of Holy Spirit.

Holy Spirit living on the inside of us and dwelling among us is the only way Heaven invades earth. He is the promise of the Father and our connection to the heavenly realm. He has been sent to abide with us forever so we must learn to abide in Him. Without Him Jesus was a man born of women. With Him Jesus became the only begotten Son of God. As the Heaven's parted, He descended upon Jesus as a dove and remained. This has become my life quest; to have Him remain.

Cultivating a New Awareness

As believers in Christ, we all have an awareness of God. Even those who do not believe Jesus is the Christ have an awareness of God. It seems to be a part of our DNA. Though we have an awareness of Him it's not always at a level we recognize. Our conscious mind seems to be unaware of His presence as we walk through our day. Cultivating a new awareness to His presence is vitally important.

During the course of training, a pilot learns to do many things. He learns how to read the gauges in the instrument panel and what to do when something isn't functioning properly. He learns how to adjust the wings during takeoff and landing. All of these are vitally important but one test they are subject to seems to be the most important to me.

As I mentioned earlier pilots are placed in a flight simulator with a note pad. The instructor then begins to reduce to oxygen levels. As this is happening the pilot is instructed to write down anything he is feeling in his body or his emotion. They continue until the level is just about low enough for the pilot to pass out. The pilot is instructed to write down on the note pad what he is feeling during this process.

Every plane has an oxygen sensor but sometimes they fail. This test trains the pilot how to use his natural senses to discern the oxygen levels in case the sensor fails. This reveals to us a truth that the writer of Hebrews brought to our attention. *But solid food belongs to those who are of full age, that is, those who by reason of use have their senses exercised to discern both good and evil.* (Hebrews 5:14).

When we are in the presence of God some part of us is aware of Him. Most of us have some way we have learned He is near. Some shake or twitch. Others cry and weep or laugh in joy. These reactions are caused when He draws near in a way we are familiar with. Discernment is vitally important. We must learn how to recognize God with all of our senses. This enables us to know Him in new ways.

Jesus was approached by both the Pharisees and Sadducees, who desired a sign, while He was in the region of Magdala. Instead of performing a miracle He rebukes them and calls them hypocrites because of their lack of discernment. *He answered and said to them, "When it is evening you say, 'It will be fair weather, for the sky is red'; "and in the morning, 'It will be foul weather today, for the sky is red and threatening.' Hypocrites! You know how to discern the face of the sky, but you cannot discern the signs of the times* (Matthew 16:2-3).

Jesus's choice of words here is quite interesting to me. He calls them hypocrites for their inability to discern. This allows us to see that they were claiming to be possessors of truth but failed to see the Truth standing in front of them. Most religious models produce a type of discernment that fails to realize God's presence when He comes in a way that is unfamiliar.

Our ability to discern spiritual atmospheres enables us to release the Kingdom in an effective way. Jesus told His disciples that the gates of hell would not prevail against them because they had keys to the Kingdom (see Matthew 16:18-19). When those verses are studied in the Greek language it paints a picture of recognizing what is available in the moment and releasing it by faith. As Holy Spirit abides within us and rests upon us we have all of Heaven's resources available to us if we can discern them.

Releasing the Kingdom

One of the greatest dangers of embracing Jesus's statement about us doing greater works is our tendency to desire methods or principles more than intimacy. When miracles happen in unusual ways many seek to understand what Kingdom principle allowed the miracle to happen rather than the one who brings Heavens reality. Most ministry is performed from the place of principles rather than from the place of intimacy with Holy Spirit.

To illustrate what I mean, there are many who send out miracle clothes and point to the principle of transferred anointing seen in Acts 19:11. I definitely believe anointing is transferred to inanimate objects but the anointing transferred was a result of Paul's passionate pursuit for the person of Jesus. The method of using a cloth is a valid method as long as Holy Spirit is choosing it.

I have found that methods come and go. The method that works for me may not work for someone else. It is best to seek an encounter with the person of God rather than a Kingdom principle when it comes to releasing the Kingdom. The examples that follow are merely examples of how the Kingdom is released. They are not designed to be rigid rules to follow.

Declaration

Outside of mankind and the animals, all of creation was spoken into existence. The universe was filled with chaos and disorder in the beginning but God brought order by declaring it. All laws that govern creation, both natural and spiritual, are active because of God's spoken word. Solomon had a unique way of expressing this truth. *Death and life are in the power of the tongue: and they that love it shall eat the fruit thereof* (Proverbs 18:21).

We see Jesus exercising this truth many times as He went about doing good. On one occasion He comes across a Centurion who has a servant in need of a miracle. *And when Jesus was entered into Capernaum, there came unto him a centurion, beseeching him, And saying, Lord, my servant lieth at home sick of the palsy, grievously tormented. And Jesus saith unto him, I will come and heal him. The centurion answered and said, Lord, I am not worthy that thou shouldest come under my roof: but speak the word only, and my servant shall be healed* (Matthew 8:5-8).

The centurion, being a man both of authority and under authority, understood that all that was needed was Jesus's command. This Centurion was noted by Jesus as having extraordinary faith because he recognized that Heaven was accessible when Jesus spoke. Having an ear to hear what Holy Spirit is saying and then declaring His message brings Heaven into earth.

The prophet Isaiah also reveals this truth to us as seen in Isaiah 51:14-16. *The captive exile hastens, that he may be loosed, That he should not die in the pit, And that his bread should not fail. But I am the LORD your God, Who divided the sea whose waves roared--The LORD of hosts is His name. And I have put My words in your mouth; I have covered you with the shadow of My hand, That I may plant the heavens, Lay the foundations of the earth, And say to Zion, 'You are My people' ".*

When it comes time to liberate those who are being held captive there are times when God reveals Himself as the general of Heaven's army. He puts His words in our mouth and then covers us with His hand. As we declare what He has placed in our mouth both the heavens and the earth begin to reflect His order. We as His representatives have the privilege of speaking on His behalf.

Benevolence

We live in a consumer society. As such, many seek better jobs so they can consume more or better things. Many feel that God's blessing is designed to only prosper them as individuals. In fact, most who attend church services reveal they attend to receive a blessing from God. That's definitely a good reason to go to church but the Kingdom operates on a much different principle. The purpose of increase in the Kingdom of Heaven is to empower those around us.

Giving is one way God's love is revealed to world. In fact, when it came time to redeem all mankind God gave His only begotten Son as an expression of His overwhelming love. Giving is somehow connected to Heavens plan of redemption for mankind. God desires to transform individuals, families, cities and nations but most times, if not always, long lasting transformation is unattainable without simple acts of kindness.

Simple acts of kindness shown to those around us are actually received as ministry to the Lord. Many see helping others as ministry to the people but Jesus sees this differently. *"Then the King will say to those on His right hand, 'Come, you blessed of My Father, inherit the kingdom prepared for you from the foundation of the world: 'for I was hungry and you gave Me food; I was thirsty and you gave Me drink; I was a stranger and you took Me in; 'I was naked and you clothed Me; I was sick and you visited Me; I was in prison and you came to Me'. "Then the righteous will answer Him, saying, 'Lord, when did we see You hungry and feed You, or thirsty and give You drink? 'When did we see You a stranger and take You in, or naked and clothe You? 'Or when did we see You sick, or in prison, and come to You?' "And the King will answer and say to them, 'Assuredly, I say to you, inasmuch as you did it to one of the least of these My brethren, you did it to Me'* (Matthew 25:34-40).

God has a world sized soft spot for the oppressed, the widow and the orphan. His heart is tender towards the poor and needy. When He releases His blessing upon a person or a group of people part of His purpose is to reach the bruised reed that has been cast aside. As recipients of His blessing we of coarse prosper as well but true riches are released when we empower those around us.

Over the years it has been amazing to see how God has blessed our family, businesses and ministries with financial increase. We of course are tithe payers and honor the Lord with the First Fruits of our increase but nothing brings my wife and I more pleasure than blessing others. It is truly amazing the difference a simple act of kindness can make when it is done as unto the Lord.

Worship

Worship is a very powerful principle. The psalmist, who wrote in an atmosphere saturated with worship, reveals to us that God enthrones praise (see Psalm 22:3). When the one true God is worshiped eventually His glory saturates the physical location where the worshipers are located. His glory always falls on the worshiper. The implication here is that worship brings His presence and the atmosphere of Heaven with it.

One of my favorite historical accounts in scripture is located in 2 Chronicles 20. King Jehoshaphat found himself in a battle that he could not win using his military power. The Ammonites, Moabites and others had chosen to destroy Judah. Knowing he couldn't win the battle without God Jehoshaphat sought Him for counsel.

God's response to Jehoshaphat and the result of his obedience is quite staggering. *And when he had consulted with the people, he appointed singers unto the LORD, and that should praise the beauty of holiness, as they went out before the army, and to say, Praise the LORD; for his mercy endureth for ever. And when they began to sing and to praise, the LORD set ambushments against the children of Ammon, Moab, and mount Seir, which were come against Judah; and they were smitten* (2 Chronicles 20:22). As the people worshiped the Lord the Kingdom was released in a way that brought defeat to the armies who were coming against Judah.

Shifting atmospheres through worship brings benefit to everyone in direct proximity of the worshipers. There were singers appointed to worship but the entire nation of Judah experienced the victory. There have been times when the Lord has instructed us as a ministry to go to different cities and areas in our city just to worship. So often we don't directly see the immediate effects but hear about them later. We later find out we were sent on an assignment to break open the atmosphere so others could move forward.

Laying on of Hands

The laying on of hands is one the foundational doctrines of the New Testament Church (see Hebrews 6:2). The transfer of anointing, baptism of the Holy Spirit and the release and the awakening of the Gifts of the Spirit are all noted as results of laying on of hands. This principle is also found in the Old Testament as the Priests would lay their hands on the scape goat. This is a great mystery to me that I don't fully understand but choose to embrace its truth anyway.

Many teach against so called "laity" laying hands on people stating that it should be reserved for the leaders of the ministry. This point of view contradicts what Jesus said about every believer. *And these signs shall follow them that believe; In my name shall they cast out devils; they shall speak with new tongues; They shall take up serpents; and if they drink any deadly thing, it shall not hurt them; they shall lay hands on the sick, and they shall recover* (Mark 6:8). Releasing the Gift of Healing through the laying on of hands is one of the results of our salvation.

One other thing I would like to mention here relates to receiving a double portion of someone's anointing by laying on of hands. Many approach well known ministers desiring a double portion of what they have. I do believe anointing can be transferred from one individual to another. I also believe in the importance of impartation but receiving a double portion by laying on of hands alone just isn't a biblical reality. The anointing operating in one individual is the same as another. The source of the anointing is the same; Holy Spirit not the individual.

History with Holy Spirit produces reliability. History is a result of relationship. The amount of anointing that is released through us is directly related to our relationship with Holy Spirit. To illustrate this point we see Paul exhorting Timothy about his unfeigned faith. Paul points to Timothy's Grandmother Lois and mother Eunice to reveal his reasoning as to his persuasion. Timothy had relationship with God, which produced similar fruits present in his mother and grandmother.

Acts of Faith

Faith and action are principles that flow together to release the Kingdom. I believe the apostle James said it best, "faith without works is dead" (see James 2:17). Though James's proclamation has a much broader application than what we will be discussing here, it is very relevant to the subject of releasing the Kingdom. Acts of faith are actions driven by faith to receive a specific breakthrough. Trying to walk on a broken foot, sowing money for a financial miracle or attempting to stand up out of a wheelchair would all be examples of acts of faith.

On His way to one of the biblical feasts, Jesus encounters a lame man at the pool of Bethesda. This man had been in his condition for thirty eight years. Coming into this knowledge Jesus asks him if he would like to be healed. The man answered saying that he can't be healed because he didn't have anyone to lower him into the pool when the angel troubled the water.

Jesus responded to this man with an impossible statement; "*Stand up, pick up your mat and walk*" (John 5:8 NLT). After hearing these words the man acted on them and was instantly healed. It is important to note that the action was directly related to needed miracle. This encounter at the pool of Bethesda reveals to us how an act of faith releases the Kingdom.

There are times when I have prayed for individuals who did not receive their miracle until there was as action to release it. When praying for people I often ask them to do what they couldn't do before the prayer. I once prayed for a woman who had broken her ankle in multiple places and had been living with pain for quite some time. She was not able to put all her weight on the ankle before so after we prayed I asked her to try to put her weight on it. As she shifted her weight the pain disappeared and she was able to put all her weight on it. I believe the action released her miracle.

One thing that must be stated here is that I am very cautious about asking someone to do something that could potential cause further damage. For example I would not ask someone with a broken leg to drop their crutches and run. I once prayed for a woman with back pain who was walking with a cane. I took her by the hand and asked her to walk with me without her cane. She took my arm to support her weight and we started walking across the front of the church. After taking two steps she took off running because the pain was gone. The simple act of faith released her miracle without endangering her in any way.

Prophetic Acts

Prophetic Acts are difficult for me to understand. Often, if not always, they are simple acts of obedience to God's voice that produce tremendous miracles. They are different than acts of faith in that the action is unrelated to the intended breakthrough. Stepping out into an isle to receive a financial miracle or walking around in a circle with a group of people to see a family member liberated in some way would be examples of prophetic acts.

During the time of Elisha the captain of Syria's army was a man named Naaman who was a leper. During one of their conquests, the army of Syria had captured an Israelite woman who became the servant of Naaman's wife. One day she informed Naaman's wife that there was a prophet who could deal with Naaman's leprosy. In response to this he ends up traveling to Samaria to visit Elisha.

Naaman comes to the place where Elisha was expecting to meet him at his door. Instead he is greeted by a messenger sent by Elisha with instructions to wash himself in the Jordan River. His expectation was for Elisha to come out and lay hands of him and call on the name of Lord but instead he was instructed to wash himself in the Jordan River. He almost missed his miracle because the pathway to his breakthrough was seemingly unrelated to his need. This simple prophetic act of washing in the river seven times healed him of an incurable disease.

On another occasion a man loses an ax head in a river. Elisha picks up a stick and casts it on the water. Amazingly this prophetic act caused the ax head to float. Being an engineer by trade I can tell you there is not a law of physics or chemistry that defines how that happened. Casting a stick on water does not change the physical properties of steel; but it this case something impossible became possible.

Special Miracles

There are times when God will release an anointing that will produce miracles that push beyond what has been seen. Jesus Himself said that those who believe in Him would produce works greater than His. Just as there are times we intentionally release the Kingdom into a circumstance, there are times when miracles happen unintentionally. These unintentional special miracles are often produced by the faith of those in need rather than the one releasing the anointing.

The apostle Peter unintentionally found himself in a shadow healing ministry (see Acts 5:15). Up to this point in the scriptures we don't read of someone's shadow producing healing; not even Jesus's. As Peter would walk by, people would be healed by his shadow without an intentional prayer or declaration. The people of the region somehow got a sense of what was available and created the opportunity for the release of miracles that had not been seen.

While in Ephesus the apostle Paul also found himself releasing special miracles (see Acts 19:11). Paul was a tent maker. The handkerchiefs and aprons that healed the sick and cast out devils were most likely ones he wore while building tents. We don't have an account where he intentionally laid his hands on his clothing and released anointing into them. As he labored to produce income, the anointing that rested upon him saturated the clothing he wore. These pieces of clothing saturated with God's presence that rested upon him as he worked produced miracles even though he wasn't present to pray or impart.

Smith Wigglesworth and Charles Finney were also men who experienced unusual miracles. Often people would cry out to God in repentance as a result of being close to them. They would get onto a passenger train or walk into a factory and revival would break out without them saying a word. These unusual miracles seen in the lives of the apostles and others throughout history are a testimony of how limitless the possibilities are when God's presence rests upon us.

In my own life there have been times when I have walked by someone in a prayer meeting or a church service and got the sense something was released only to hear the testimony later. I have breathed on individuals and they were healed. Other times I have had waiters in restaurants ask me to pray for them without me mentioning to them I was a Christian. The Kingdom is within us. We are the gate of Heaven. As we allow Holy Spirit to rest upon us everywhere we go we carry with us unlimited possibilities. As I have grown into this understanding I expect Heaven to invade earth everywhere I go whether intentional or unintentional.

Chapter 9

Naturally Supernatural

At the time of Christ there was a new ideology that dominated the global powers that ruled the modern world. This new ideology began to emerge during the time of Socrates and others who led the way in philosophical thought. The ancient Greeks gave the world a new way of thinking as they searched within themselves for answers. Basically the Greeks worshiped mankind and were the initiators of what we call Humanism.

By the time of the New Testament, many Greeks didn't believe in their Greek gods but instead created gods in the form of man. They were of the opinion that they had the power within themselves to reach the apex of human existence. They felt they didn't need any input from any form of deity because they themselves were their own gods. They felt they could make the world a perfect place if everyone just worked together.

The Greeks were the innovators of the democratic government. They believed that this form of government would allow peace to rule and all would enjoy utopia. There are many today who hold to this way of thinking and seek world peace through human efforts of self-governing. An example of this can be seen when our government attempted to bring a resolution to the Middle East by establishing a democracy in Gaza.

America and the other nations of the world stood in amazement when the Palestinians elected terrorists to rule this newly founded democracy in Gaza. Operating in a Greek mindset, America tried to impose a democracy on a people who live in a world dominated by fear. Once they were given the power to rule themselves they chose terror and not peace. Human efforts only produce natural solutions that fall dramatically short of Gods plan for man to rule supernaturally as He rules.

The Greek Mindset

The main theme and operating principle of the Greek mindset is pride that arises from a humanistic intellectual world view. The Greeks believed knowledge was power and many people today feel the same way. Intellectuals feel if they can understand how something occurs, then the outcome can be changed and manipulated to get a desired result. This mindset is in direct conflict with Heaven's model which is naturally supernatural.

An individual operating in a Greek mindset wants to make sure everything makes sense intellectually and that it is done by the book. The Greek worldview society is a much more pleasant place to live than a society that is ruled by terrorism and fear such as Pakistan. Though this is true, the Kingdom of God awakens creative purpose and brings peace that crushes the head of the serpent.

Individuals living with a Greek mindset view God as distant and non-relational in nature. Rather than seeking Him relationally and allowing Him to reveal Himself in the scriptures, the bible is read as an educational book. Theology and doctrine are used to reason out truth using the human intellect. This approach is very systematic and most times doesn't take into consideration what Holy Spirit is saying now. There is no room for the supernatural so men are left to their own devices.

Success in the Greek culture is measured mainly by the level of knowledge one possess. Education and intellectual knowledge becomes the answer when failure is experienced. If we were to walk the streets in any city in America and ask people how one improves their quality of life in most cases the answer would be go to college and get a degree.

Education is a great thing that gives us tools to better understand our physical world. I myself have a Bachelor's degree in Petroleum Engineering but without God's favor in my life I have no way to experience success using Heaven's measuring stick. Heaven's model of success is directly related to how much of God's nature we have taken on. As we turn to the Lord a new world is opened up to us as we see Him. Then Holy Spirit transforms us supernaturally into the image we see (see 2 Corinthians 3:18).

Most church's today hold to cessation theology that states the gifts of the Spirit are no longer in operation. Many Christians believe this and feel that human reasoning reigns supreme. Because of this, many fail to see that God operates by His Spirit. If we are going to walk with God by faith then we must operate by His Spirit and allow Him to lead us in all truth.

It was never God's initial intent for man to rule without His direct interaction. We do not have the ability to live in God's best without His direction. There is not a self-help book on the market today that will get us there. Democracy is a wonderful form of human government but God's Kingdom Government is much better.

Reason and intellectual thought are profitable but there are things within God's Kingdom that are far more advanced than any human intellect can comprehend. The foolishness of the Kingdom confounds the wisdom of this world. There will be times when we will have to do things that just don't make sense...it's called operating by faith.

The Practical Side of the Supernatural

We were created to be naturally supernatural, ruling in the earth supernaturally as God rules in the heavens. Not instead of God but because of God. We rule with Him as we come into agreement with Heaven's order. Jesus is perfect theology and He walked the earth as a man supernaturally empowered by Holy Spirit. He is our example and prototype.

As we study Jesus's life and teachings we are able to gain insights into how we activate the Kingdom within us. Fasting and prayer are both seen in His life and revealed as a way we deal with the works of the devil. Worship and devotion are also seen in His life and found in His commandments. Giving and performing simple acts of kindness are also seen. These are all ways we cultivate our relationship with Him and create a continual connection to Him through Holy Spirit.

Our Daily Sacrifice

Time is one of our most valuable resources. In fact I would venture to say that it is our most important resource. Money comes and goes as do intellectual ideas but time is the only resource we can't get back if we lose it…or can we? In God's blueprint for blessing He gave us a model we can look to in order to capitalize on every moment of our precious time. Built in this process is a plan of restoration that allows us to make up what has been lost and be accelerated to what He has intended for us. This process begins by understanding how to interact with Him on a daily basis.

In Exodus 20:24 God spoke to Moses and told him to build an altar of earth. God told him that if he built an altar and offered burnt offerings and peace offerings on it He would then meet with him there, speak to him and bless him. What an awesome promise! If we set ourselves apart as an altar of earth and offer our lives to God as a living sacrifice then we have a promise that He will meet with us, speak to us and bless us!

When the Lord instructed Moses to build the Tabernacle there was one specific offering known as the morning and evening sacrifice. Exodus 29:38 says, *"Now this is what you shall offer on the altar: two lambs of the first year, day by day continually. One lamb you shall offer in the morning and the other lamb you shall offer at twilight"*. Every day two lambs were offered on the altar they built for the Lord, one in the morning and one in the evening.

This morning and evening sacrifice is also mentioned in Exodus 30:6-7 which says, *"Every morning when Aaron maintains the lamps, he must burn fragrant incense on the altar. And each evening when he lights the lamps, he must again burn incense in the LORD's presence. This must be done from generation to generation".* The offering was given to the Lord in the place where He promised He would meet with the givers of the offering in the morning and in the evening. This instruction was not only for the generation of Moses but from generation to generation.

Under the New Covenant we are not required to bring a lamb of the first year but we become a living sacrifice offered unto the Lord. As we present ourselves to the Lord, once in the morning and once in the evening we have a promise that He will meet with us, speak to us and bless us. There are no minimum time requirements for this. Allow the Holy Spirit to set your times. Some days it may be as little as five minutes and others it may be an hour or more.

During these times I encourage you to have your bible readily available with a notebook and something to write with because you will find that God is quick to honor His promise. I also encourage you to play worship music and spend a few minutes quite before the Lord. You will find that your days take on a new dimension as Holy Spirit fills you with faith and power. Your nights will be restful as He restores your strength while you sleep in His presence.

I would like to offer you some more thoughts about worship, fasting, prayer, devotion and giving. I will also give you some of my methods just as an example for you to look at rather than a formula to success. We all have different family dynamics and one method does not fit all. It is important that we seek Holy Spirit in this and allow Him to lead us. He will reveal to you the model that best activates the Kingdom in your life.

Worship

Worship is one of my highest values. I live to worship. Some of you may not be as systematic as I am in your approach to God but most times I set aside time just to be with Him. My goal is just to spend time in His presence as the object of His love. Sometimes I will play music and sing praises to Him. Other times I will sit quietly and not say a word. Again my goal is not to pray through a list or specifically seek answers; my goal is to spend time with Him as the object of His love.

The scripture declares very clearly that our Father inhabits the praises of His people. When I worship Him He is present. Sometimes I am not aware of His manifest presence but I know He is there. Other times His power so fills the atmosphere there is no doubt He is in the room. Either way I speak to Him and enjoy Him. Jesus declared that we are no longer servants but friends so I make it a point to cultivate this intimate friendship with my creator (see John 15:15).

Some might feel this approach negates God's sovereignty and holiness but it His idea not mine. My viewpoint of my position in the world does not change. I am fully aware He is holy and all I have in God finds its origins in Christ. As I speak and commune with Him I thank Him for allowing me such a privilege; to be a joint-heir with Christ.

Speaking with God as a friend as I worship Him does not cause me to be disobedient or reject His counsel. I worship Him as El Elyon, the Most High God, and He invites me commune with Him as His friend. Worship shifts atmospheres and brings His power in corporate gatherings that allows us to release breakthrough but at home in our personal time it should be all about cultivating our friendship with Him. As we walk with Him in worship we become like Him.

Biblically worship is much more than signing a song, playing an instrument, the raising of hands or kneeling or lying before God. Everything is seen as worship to the Lord (see Colossians 3:17). It is important to make this distinction to gain the correct biblical view of worship in order to unlock its power.

Most Christians see the world with a clear divide between sacred and secular. Anything that is not deemed Christian falls into the category of secular. This is an illegal divide under the New Covenant. The work we do in the Church on Sunday morning is not more sacred than the work we do in the market place Monday thru Friday. God's presence is just as accessible in the market place as it is in a local Church. All we do should be done as an offering of worship to the Lord thus inviting His fire to fall on us as living sacrifice.

Prayer

Jesus had much to say about prayer. It is a crucial part of fellowshipping with our Father in Heaven. Over the years I have read many books on prayer and have implemented many different methods. I have found that my prayer methods have continued to change but my focus has remained the same; to commune with my Father in Heaven. It is not my desire to reveal to you what I believe is the most effective prayer model but just to share my method.

Praying in the Spirit is one of my great joys and is my main method. I am so thankful for the gift of praying in other tongues. I find great comfort in the fact that I can pray the perfect will of God when I am empowered by Holy Spirit (see Romans 8:26). He knows exactly what I need to be strengthened to perform His will. He also builds up my faith and empowers me to remain in His love (see Jude 1:20).

As I pray in the Spirit, I gain the ability to pray with understanding. Jesus informed us that our Father knows what we need before we ask. For many this verse is interpreted as taking our list to Him and asking even though He knows what we need. Those who hold to this interpretation further state that He is omniscient and already knows but we have to ask anyway. I do believe this has merit but I think it is better interpreted to mean that He knows what I need so I should allow Him to create my list rather than bringing one to Him.

My prayer time doesn't consist of building a list of needs and desires and then presenting my case to the heavenly court. I pray in the Spirit and allow Him to reveal to me my Fathers heart and then I declare His will be done in the earth as it is in Heaven. I also watch over my desires when I am praying knowing He will give me the desires of my heart (see Mark 11:24).

Prayer is a beautiful gift of communication that enables us to connect with our Fathers heart as He connects with ours. I find that many times He is very interested in how I feel about the affairs of my life and those around me. This allows me to see that He does not want me to be a robot that is programmed to obey orders. He wants me to be a son who dreams His dreams. We see this kind of interaction in the lives of Abraham, Isaac, Jacob, Moses, Joshua, Joseph, Daniel and many others found in the bible.

As you commune with Holy Spirit in prayer, I encourage you to still your heart and rest in Him. If your mind starts to wander you don't have to rebuke the devil or feel like you are not being effective. Our Father is concerned about what you are concerned about and most likely He is giving you an opportunity to find solutions to your concerns. If you start thinking about something going on at work or a personal situation get a pen and paper and write down your concerns and wait for answers.

Many feel that if they lose focus, or at least the focus they have brought into their prayer time, they have failed. God has a way of bringing to our attention what is important in the moment. Often times it relates to what we are currently experiencing in our daily affairs. Holy Spirit holds the position of convicting me when I am off track and I have found that He is much better at that job than I am. If I convict myself because I feel I am not performing well then I become rather hopeless. When He brings conviction to my heart it leaps with joy because it comes with enabling power to accomplish what is needed.

Fasting

Fasting is a mystery that I really don't fully understand. I do however know by Jesus's instruction and by experience that it is needed and effective. One area that I believe we often fail when fasting is not allowing to Lord to choose our fast. There has been a cultural phenomenon in American church culture known as the "Daniel Fast". Many churches begin the year with twenty one days of selective fasting.

I believe this is a great idea. Any fasting is better than none but we must be careful to seek Holy Spirit in our planning. Many deem one method over another as the correct one but I don't think the method is the Lord's concern. I believe the purpose behind our fasting is really what He is concerned about.

The words of the prophet Isaiah rebuking the people of Israel are truly shocking to me when I read them. *"Shout with the voice of a trumpet blast. Shout aloud! Don't be timid. Tell my people Israel of their sins! Yet they act so pious! They come to the Temple every day and seem delighted to learn all about me. They act like a righteous nation that would never abandon the teachings of its God. They ask me to take action on their behalf, pretending they want to be near me. 'We have fasted before you!' they say. 'Why aren't you impressed? We have been very hard on ourselves, and you don't even notice it!' 'I will tell you why!' I respond. 'It's because you are fasting to please yourselves. Even while you fast, you keep oppressing your workers. What good is fasting when you keep on fighting and quarreling? This kind of fasting will never get you anywhere with me."* (Isaiah 58:1-4 NLT).

One thing we must keep in mind in Isaiah's words is that the people were fasting on the days they were instructed to according to the Law of Moses. The problem was it had become a religious activity that lacked relationship and purpose outside of themselves. *"You humble yourselves by going through the motions of penance, bowing your heads like reeds bending in the wind. You dress in burlap and cover yourselves with ashes. Is this what you call fasting? Do you really think this will please the LORD? "No, this is the kind of fasting I want: Free those who are wrongly imprisoned; lighten the burden of those who work for you. Let the oppressed go free, and remove the chains that bind people. Share your food with the hungry, and give shelter to the homeless. Give clothes to those who need them, and do not hide from relatives who need your help"* (Isaiah 58:5-7 NLT).

Fasting as a religious exercise, along with any other form of pious activity for that matter, is not pleasing to God. When we finish, all we have accomplished is becoming hungry. Jesus was led by Holy Spirit into the wilderness to fast for forty days. I don't think the number of days He fasted is the nugget of truth but the fact that it was Holy Spirit that led Him. He overcame the devil's temptations in the wilderness and then came out filled with power to destroy his works because He followed Holy Spirits leading.

When we fast our focus should not be becoming more spiritual. Denying ourselves food is a small part but most if not all fasting is done by not eating. According to Isaiah's words simple acts of kindness and choosing to give your employees a raise rather than yourself are acceptable as fasting. If Holy Spirit instructs you not to eat a meal then buy one for someone who can't. When we afflict our souls as the scripture teaches us we should be bringing freedom to those who are in captivity. Enabling and empowering those around us by destroying the works of the devil should be our focus.

Devotion

The Holy Scriptures are filled with life. The Bible isn't a history book even though it is filled with many historical accounts. It is also not a book of solutions even though we find many in it. It is simply God's teaching that enables us to draw closer to Him. His teaching is not designed to bring us all the answers per say but is an invitation that allows us to experience His glory and to become like Him. In fact as I read most times I have more questions than I started with before beginning reading. The writer of Proverbs states this truth well when he said, *"It is the glory of God to conceal a thing; but it is the glory of kings to search out a matter"* (Proverbs 25:2).

As we walk through the aisles of our favorite Christian book store we find entire sections filled with devotionals. We have devotionals for teens, devotionals for young adults, devotionals for parents, both single and married. We have devotionals for every demographic group in existence today but yet we still seem to make it an intellectual exercise rather than a life filled experience with Holy Spirit.

Many hold the scriptures in higher regard than the one who inspired them. It's as if they see the godhead as being Father, Son and Holy Bible. Please don't misunderstand me as I cherish the Bible and believe that it is the authority in truth. My point is that the person of

God is not found in the scriptures themselves. They are not designed to bring the answer directly but to bring us into a supernatural encounter with the one who has them.

Jesus rebuked the religious leaders of His day informing them that eternal life is not found in the scriptures but in Him (see John 5:39). As we read through the Bible we should begin to see Jesus as Holy Spirit reveals Him to us. The scriptures themselves hold value but outside of Christ we are still bound by this natural world. When we see Jesus by revelation everything changes. The words written come alive within us as Holy Spirit transforms us into the image we see.

Before I open my bible I always pray and ask Holy Spirit to lead me in truth. Most times I don't have a specific regimen I hold to but I just open and start reading. I certainly don't take issue with any form of structured reading like the Bible in a Year or any other devotional. Again I don't think the method is as important as having Holy Spirit reveal the truth of what is being read. The point is that we should be reading a bible and allowing Holy Spirit to reveal to us its truth.

As far as translations are concerned I can't say I have an overall preferred translation as they all give me the raw materials I need. I do have preferences I use for different reasons, such as general reading or word study. I don't feel it's important to inform you of my preferences because no matter what translation I am reading Holy Spirit reveals to me the blueprint I need to properly apply the material. Without Him all I have is raw material. With Him I have the blueprint.

Giving

As we discussed earlier, giving is a very important aspect of our lives as Christians. I like to think of it from the perspective of honor. There is something about showing honor that activates restoration and causes the devil to release his grip. I believe it is a direct expression of biblical love. The most displayed bible verse in our culture reveals this truth. God so loved the world He gave His only begotten son (John 3:16).

The scriptures clearly reveal to us three ways we are supposed to give. We are instructed to honor the Lord with the tithe, the first fruit and to give to the poor. Many are engaged in the process of giving but are missing one or more of these keys that unlock the door to walking in true Biblical blessing and prosperity. It is Gods will and good pleasure to bless us but we must meet His requirements. In the Bible God gave us His requirements for abundant blessing.

Faith is the most important aspect of our giving. Without faith it is impossible to please God. Many give out of tradition rather than faith. The next thing we must do is be cheerful in our giving, which is a work of the Spirit that manifests when we give in faith. We must also be walking in love, as the Apostle Paul exhorts us that if we give everything but fail to give love then it is unprofitable. Before we begin speaking about tithing, first fruits and benevolence we must understand that all three stem from the root of faith, love and cheerfulness.

The Tithe

In the scripture the Hebrew word used for tithe is mahasar, which means the tenth part. Leviticus 27:30-32 states, *"And all the tithe of the land, whether of the seed of the land, or of the fruit of the tree, is the LORD'S: it is holy unto the LORD. And if a man will at all redeem ought of his tithes, he shall add thereto the fifth part thereof. And concerning the tithe of the herd, or of the flock, even of whatsoever passeth under the rod, the tenth shall be holy unto the LORD."* The tithe represents ten percent of all of our increase and it is holy to the Lord.

I have heard many times from many individuals that the tithe is an Old Testament thing and we are under the New Covenant and aren't required to pay tithe. Though this argument may sound convincing it is not biblical. In Mathew 23:23 Jesus makes this statement to the religious leaders of the time, *"Woe unto you, scribes and Pharisees, hypocrites! for ye pay tithe of mint and anise and cummin, and have omitted the weightier matters of the law, judgment, mercy, and faith: these ought ye to have done, and not to leave the other undone."* They were to focus on the weightier matters of God's teaching but notice he says not to leave the other, paying their tithe, undone.

We see another occasion in Mark 12:17 where Jesus is confronted by the Pharisees and the Herodians with a question about paying taxes to Caesar. In His answer to them He says, *And Jesus answering said unto them, "Render to Caesar the things that are Caesar's, and to God the things that are God's".* Jesus once again sets the standard for us to render to God His portion. These are two occasions where we are exhorted to pay tithe by the one who established the New Covenant.

If we choose not to honor the Lord with His portion then we find ourselves living under a curse. *You are cursed with a curse, for ye have robbed me, even this whole nation* (Malachi 3:9). This verse reveals to us that if we do not pay our tithes then we are robbing God of His portion and cannot live in abundance.

The good news is that God promises us great blessing if we honor Him. *Bring ye all the tithes into the storehouse, that there may be meat in mine house, and prove me now herewith, saith the LORD of hosts, if I will not open you the windows of heaven, and pour you out a blessing, that there shall not be room enough to receive it. And I will rebuke the devourer for your sakes, and he shall not destroy the fruits of your ground; neither shall your vine cast her fruit before the time in the field, saith the LORD of hosts. And all nations shall call you blessed: for ye shall be a delightsome land, saith the LORD of hosts* (Malachi 3:10-11). There is a promise for great increase but we must honor the Lord with our tithes.

The tithe opens up a powerful blessing; the Lord promised He would open the windows of heaven and pour out an uncontainable blessing. He would also rebuke the devourer for our sakes and our labors will be fruitful and prosperous. If we pay our tithes we gain access to the open window blessing and sustained increase. This is the first aspect of our giving; we must bring in a tenth of all our increase.

The First Fruit

The first fruit offering is probably the most misunderstood biblical offering listed in the scripture. Often times we have heard of the first fruit in the context of the tithe but they are two separate offerings. The tithe is a tenth of all of our increase. It was not examined to eliminate a portion deemed unfit to offer to God. This is not true of the first fruit offering. It was a special offering that was the first of the increase and the best of the increase. Unlike the tithe this offering needed to be examined for impurities to insure it was the best.

The Hebrew word for first fruit is reshiyth, which means first, beginning or best. It is also used to describe a chief or the head. The first fruit offering represents the first increase of its kind. Exodus 23:19 says, *"The first of the firstfruits of thy land thou shalt bring into the house of the LORD thy God. Thou shalt not seethe a kid in his mother's milk".* Leveticus 23:10-11 says, *"Speak unto the children of Israel, and say unto them, When ye be come into the land which I give unto you, and shall reap the harvest thereof, then ye shall bring a sheaf of the firstfruits of your harvest unto the priest: And he shall wave the sheaf before the LORD, to be accepted for you: on the morrow after the sabbath the priest shall wave it.* It is important to notice that there isn't a specific amount placed on this offering like the tithe. It's about quality and sequence rather than quantity.

There is a very specific blessing that goes along with the first fruit that is not obtained by paying tithe alone. *Honour the LORD with thy substance, and with the firstfruits of all thine increase: So shall thy barns be filled with plenty, and thy presses shall burst out with new wine* (Proverbs

3:9). Honoring the Lord with the first of our increase allows our barns to be filled with plenty and gives us access to NEW wine. This is a New Covenant principle. *For if the firstfruit be holy, the lump is also holy: and if the root be holy, so are the branches* (Romans 11:16). If we give God our first and our best then He will bless the rest!

The first fruit is a special offering that is brought to the Lord at the beginning of every month. It represents the first of its kind of all our increase. This would relate to a raise, a promotion, a bonus, an inheritance or any other form of increase that is the first of its kind to you. There may be times that you don't necessarily have an increase that is the first of its kind but you can always give the Lord your best.

To make this practical let's use a couple of examples. Let's say your monthly paycheck is $2500 and you receive a raise of $100 per month. The first month you receive your raise your paycheck will be $2600. On the first of the next month you take that first $100, because it is the first of its kind, and offer it to the Lord as your first fruit. Then pay tithe on the rest like you always have. So your giving would reflect something like this: $100 as First Fruit and $250 as Tithe. After that your tithe would be $260 or ten percent of your total increase and the first fruit would be whatever value the Lord instructs you to give.

When the first of the month comes around again you may not have gotten another raise or any type of increase that is the first of its kind but you can give your best. I always ask the Lord what He requires of me as my first fruit and He is faithful to tell me. The next month your giving may look something like this: Your pay was $2600 so your tithe would be $260 and your first fruit may be $25, $50, $150 or whatever value the Lord instructs you to give. Remember this value isn't a specific amount like the tithe but represents your first and your best.

There is also a Feast of Fruit Fruits where we give a special offering for the year (see Leviticus 23:9-14). This feast is held after Passover during the biblical month of Nisan, which normally falls sometime during March or April on our calendar. Around the time of Easter you may want to give your first paycheck or any other amount the Lord has instructed you to give. You will want to ask Him what He would like you to give and wave it before Him during the feast time. This will ensure that the remainder of your year will be blessed. If you honor the Lord with your best He will bless the rest.

Benevolence

The final aspect of our giving is found in Leviticus 23:22. *And when ye reap the harvest of your land, thou shalt not make clean riddance of the corners of thy field when thou reapest, neither shalt thou gather any gleaning of thy harvest: thou shalt leave them unto the poor, and to the stranger: I am the LORD your God.* Once God allows us to experience our harvest we help those who are less fortunate than we are. This is a very important key to our giving.

In the Gospels, Jesus tells a parable that we have come to know as the Good Samaritan. In this parable, He is illustrating the importance of being mindful of our fellow man and that turning aside to help those in need is an important aspect of His Kingdom. When Jesus made the statement for us to seek first the Kingdom and His righteousness He was in one sense speaking to this aspect of God's heart. Biblically speaking one sense of righteousness is linked with simple acts of kindness towards those who are less fortunate than we are. Jesus was letting us know that seeking a Kingdom harvest is directly linked with helping the widow, the orphan and the oppressed.

Deuteronomy 24:19 reveals the blessing that comes with honoring this principle. *When thou cuttest down thine harvest in thy field, and hast forgot a sheaf in the field, thou shalt not go again to fetch it: it shall be for the stranger, for the fatherless, and for the widow: that the LORD thy God may bless thee in all the work of thine hands.* When we help the stranger, the fatherless and the widow God ensures that all the works of our hands are blessed.

As we continue in the text God reveals His reasoning for commanding this principle. *When thou beatest thine olive tree, thou shalt not go over the boughs again: it shall be for the stranger, for the fatherless, and for the widow. When thou gatherest the grapes of thy vineyard, thou shalt not glean it afterward: it shall be for the stranger, for the fatherless, and for the widow. And thou shalt remember that thou wast a bondman in the land of Egypt: therefore I command thee to do this thing* (Deuteronomy 24:20-22). We are instructed to honor this form of giving so that we are reminded that we were once in a place of captivity.

When we bring our tithes into God's storehouse then we have a promise of an open heaven and the devourer is rebuked. When we honor the Lord with the first fruits of our increase we have a promise that our barns will be filled with plenty and our vats will be overflowing with new wine. When we seek ways to help the fatherless, the widow, the stranger or anyone who is less fortunate than we are then we are assured the works of our hands will be blessed.

The Kingdom of God is not moved or predicated by need but is activated by faith through a covenant promise. Living in blessing and experiencing harvest is the will and the good pleasure of our Father but we must meet His conditions. That said, we must remember that our motivation for giving flows from our relationship with Him. We give because we love Him. We love Him because we believe He loves us. We believe He loves us because He is alive within us; Christ the hope of glory.

Chapter 10

We Are a Living Sacrifice

The Old Testament is saturated with offerings and sacrifices. The instructions we read are renowned for their many and complicated details. As foreign as this sacrificial system is to our Western culture, it has great significance pertaining to living a life in His presence. Even before Moses spoke with God at Sinai, offerings and sacrifices were a major part of the practice of relationship with God. Cain and Abel, Noah and the patriarchs, Jethro the priest of Median and many others offered sacrifice before the tabernacle was built.

Offerings and sacrifice remained central to God's people throughout history. The ritual systems of Moses's Tabernacle are also seen in the first and second temples but before the first temple was constructed by Solomon something changed. King David, God's second chosen king, established a tabernacle furnished with just one thing; the Ark of the Covenant. Though there were many burnt offerings offered on the altar outside the tent those appointed to serve inside offered no burnt offering.

The Offering Made by Fire

Burnt offerings were a major aspect of God's system of worship. I spoke of the morning and evening sacrifice earlier which was offered both at the entrance of the Holy Place and Holy of Holies. In both places, God promised that He would manifest Himself when the offerings were made. This burnt offering that was offered on the altar in the inner court and on the altar of incense in the Holy Place were said to be offerings made by fire.

I often wondered why God would make it a point to inform us that these burnt offerings were offerings made by fire. To me, saying that it is a burnt offering is sufficient enough for us to see that it was an offering made by fire. The fact that God would take the time to state the obvious reveals to me that the true meaning wasn't as obvious as it appeared. There was a deeper meaning to His instruction that reaches beyond the way these burnt offerings were offered.

The offering brought to be burned on the altar had to meet strict requirements. As important as these characteristics were they seem to be secondary to the real requirement. The offering wasn't acceptable to God as a sweet smelling savor until it was consumed by the fire on the altar. As the smoke rose from the altar the offering was complete. The character of the offering only qualified it to be placed on the altar. The fire that consumed it made it into an acceptable offering.

I believe the Old Testament reveals to us the power of sin and our need for a savior. Along this line of thinking I believe the fire on the altar was a sign of God's judgment on sin. His fire fell from Heaven and consumed the offering revealing to the people that it was accepted (see Leviticus 9:24-26). The fire of the Old Testament was a picture of His judgment which consumed the wages of sin; namely death.

Just as the Old Testament reveals to us the power of sin, the life of Jesus reveals to us the power of grace. Under the Old Covenant a person with leprosy was deemed unclean and any who came in contact with that person was also deemed unclean. However, when Jesus came in contact with those consumed with leprosy the opposite happened. Instead of Him contracting the disease those who were once consumed by sickness were now consumed by His healing grace.

Everyone Jesus came in contact with experienced the power of the grace that rested upon Him. As I have stated many times I believe it was Holy Spirit resting upon him and living within Him that enabled Him to walk the earth as He did. Just like the offerings brought to the door of the inner court and the Holiest of Holy's, He met the strict requirements of the Law. Once He arose from the waters of the river Jordan the fire revealing God's acceptance fell upon Him in the form of a dove.

The Baptism of Fire

John the Baptist, named as the greatest prophet who ever lived by Jesus, saw Holy Spirit descend upon Him and remain. Before John baptized Jesus he pleaded with Him desiring His baptism (see Matthew 3:14). This is quite profound to me because John was said to have the "spirit of Elijah", who called fire from Heaven. Every other prophet alive before him saw his day a far off but he beheld the Lamb of God and revealed Him to the world.

The instruction John was given to reveal the one he was looking for is quite interesting to me. *I didn't know he was the one, but when God sent me to baptize with water, he told me, "The one on whom you see the Spirit descend and rest is the one who will baptize with the Holy Spirit"* (John 1:33 NLT). The Father gave John one simple qualifier to identify the one who was coming to represent Him perfectly in the earth. The one whom he saw the Spirit descend upon and rest would be the only begotten of the Father.

When questioned by the religious leaders of the time about whom he was, John declared to them that there was one coming after him who would baptize with the Holy Spirit and fire. At this moment in time he did not speak of Jesus as the Lamb of God, the King of Kings, the Mighty God or the Prince of Peace. Later he would declare Jesus as the Lamb of God but here he specifically mentions that Jesus was coming to baptize with Holy Spirit and fire.

John used the Greek word *baptizo* to describe how Jesus was going to release the Holy Spirit and fire. *Baptizo* means to immerse or submerge. He was coming to allow our lives to be totally immersed by Holy Spirit. The fire was coming from Heaven but this time instead of consuming a lifeless sacrifice it was going to fall on earthen vessels who were very much alive. This baptism of fire was coming to do what the Law was unable to do. Even though the Law is glorious it cannot purge our conscience of dead works and transform us into children of God.

The idea of being baptized by fire has been seen as a very negative experience in our Western Culture. When it is mentioned, people are speaking of sending someone into something ill equipped so that failure is certain. The opposite is true however. When the fire of Holy Spirit falls upon us it is a sign of God's acceptance of Jesus's payment for our sin. He quickens our mortal body and resurrects our spirit. When He fills us and rests upon us we become a new creation equipped and enabled to fulfill our destiny; to destroy the works of the devil.

Holy Spirit descending and resting upon a man was different than any other time in history. In times past, Holy Spirit would descend upon a man or woman to release God's anointing to deliver the people but never do we see the Spirit resting on someone. I do believe that Moses, Joseph, Daniel, Isaiah, Elijah, Elisha and others experienced a measure of this but not a continual resting of God's presence.

History does tell us that God's presence rested upon the Ark of the Covenant and remained. This was a shadow revealing the one who was coming who the Spirit would descend upon and rest. The shittim wood overlaid with gold that made up the Ark of the Covenant was a picture of Christ; a man born of woman shaped and molded by Holy Spirit. It was the fire of Holy Spirit that resurrected Jesus and enabled Him to accomplish all He was sent to accomplish. It was also the fire of Holy Spirit descending upon those is the upper room on the Day of Pentecost that accomplished the same thing.

This baptism of fire forever changed the lives of those He descended upon on that day and those He continues to descend upon. Many feel it is impossible to walk in the same anointing the Apostles and disciples did as seen in the book of Acts but I disagree. The Spirit that rested upon them is the same Spirit that is available today. He is given without measure. I believe the key that unlocks the same kind of manifestation today is given Him a place to remain.

Our Reasonable Service

When writing to the church in Rome Paul exhorts them to present themselves to God as a living sacrifice. He states that this is our reasonable service to Him (see Romans 12:1). Many hold to a theology that relates this service to our spiritual disciplines such as prayer, fasting, devotion and good works. Most sermons I have heard relating to this verse point to the fruits of the Spirit being our goal but I think we miss the most crucial aspect of what Paul was communicating here.

The preceding chapter reveals that because Israel chose their traditions over Jesus the other nations of the world could now be reconciled to Him. Paul is very clear in his communication that the promise of God was not fulfilled by meeting the requirements of the Law but by grace. Our reasonable service to God is not our ability to discipline ourselves through religious practices. As we live a life consumed by the flames of Holy Spirit we become the living sacrifice that is made by fire.

The prophet Malachi reveals this mystery to us as he brings God's final plea to His people. *"Look! I am sending my messenger, and he will prepare the way before me. Then the Lord you are seeking will suddenly come to his Temple. The messenger of the covenant, whom you look for so eagerly, is surely coming," says the LORD of Heaven's Armies. But who will be able to endure it when he comes? Who will be able to stand and face him when he appears? For he will be like a blazing fire that refines metal, or like a strong soap that bleaches clothes. He will sit like a refiner of silver, burning away the dross. He will purify the Levites, refining them like gold and silver, so that they may once again offer acceptable sacrifices to the LORD. Then once more the LORD will accept the offerings brought to him by the people of Judah and Jerusalem, as he did in the past"* (Malachi 3:1-4 ASV).

The Lord is only accepting offerings brought to Him by those who have experienced the refiner's fire. With this understanding I believe the apostle Paul was revealing to us that the Father's love for us qualifies us to receive Holy Spirit because Jesus paid the ultimate price. We become a living sacrifice when Holy Spirit quickens our mortal bodies and resurrects our spirit. I believe it is quite arrogant and prideful to think that any other offering or sacrifice is more sufficient than Jesus to allow us to be accepted by God.

For many it may seem confusing that our reasonable service to God is to allow Holy Spirit to refine us. It is His refining that transforms us into His image and enables us not to be conformed to this world. It is His flames of passion that awaken both His gifts and fruits. Our ability to heal the sick, cast our devils, walk in love or be filled with hope cannot be cultivated any other way. After all they are the qualities of the person of Holy Spirit and not our human qualities.

We Are a Living Sacrifice

Humanism has overrun our churches in America. Much that is considered to be sacrifice in the church today is done out of human efforts. Many reject the supernatural attributes of Holy Spirit in fear of being deceived not realizing they are deceived already. They embrace a set of principles or values and call it sacrifice. Disciplines are then exercised in an attempt to cultivate habits that will allow them to enjoy a better quality of life. Disciplines are important as are good habits but all of these must revolve around Holy Spirit. He is the one who enables us to fulfill our reasonable service to God; to be a living sacrifice.

Our human efforts to cultivate a better quality of life always lead to confusion and failure. We are unable to accomplish our creative purposes by looking inwardly for hope or will power. The mind that has not been renewed by Holy Spirit is actually warring against its own creative purpose. We must remember that Jesus said He could do nothing of Himself (see John 5:30). He didn't look inwardly, He looked to the Father through the eyes of Holy Spirit. He was perfect and without sin yet He still depended on Holy Spirit to enable Him to accomplish what He came to do; to destroy the works of the devil.

We were created with glory and honor. Our purpose in this life is to rule in the earth as our Father rules in the Heavens. Our destiny is to become like our master and destroy the works of the devil. As we search for the Kingdom of Heaven within Holy Spirit then we become a living sacrifice. Through Him, we are transformed into supernatural beings who possess the same authority Jesus was given. Through Him, we are able to walk in the same power that Jesus walked in. This only happens through encounter.

We as individuals must have a supernatural encounter with Holy Spirit. The principles of the Kingdom are merely seeds that must be watered by Holy

Spirit to bring forth the desired fruit. A Kingdom principle without an encounter with the King is like having a vehicle without having the keys. The vehicle has great potential to do what it was designed to do but without the keys there is no power to enable it. The keys supply the power that enables the engine to transfer its energy to the wheels.

Jesus said that He would give us the keys to the Kingdom. He said that the gates of hell would not be able to prevail against us. Many claim to have the keys but are not experiencing the victory Jesus promised. I have been in that very same situation myself many times. When I find myself without victory I have learned that I am not in need of another method but another encounter with the King. This has become my life's passion; to continually have a supernatural encounter with the King.

I pray that what you have read ignites a fire on the inside of you to pursue more. I pray that the eyes of your understanding would be opened to see the King of Glory. When you see Him you will begin to become like Him. The world around you will benefit greatly as His purposes are awakened within you. The Lord will bless you and keep. His face will shine upon you and He will give you peace in Jesus name!

About the Author

Michael L. Ruegamer, Senior Leader of Freedom House Apostolic Center, is an impactful, spiritual authority whose mission is to bring transformation to individuals, families, communities and nations. He is an anointed teacher and a dynamic preacher with a life changing message of transformation and empowerment. Michael's desire is to empower the Body of Christ to overcome and experience the reality of living a life filled with God's presence.

With over 10 years of experience, Michael's ministry includes a wide range of spiritual gifts. Along with his wife, he founded Mantles of Destiny International Ministries, Freedom House Apostolic Center and Unveiled Conference Ministries. Together they have developed training programs designed to empower individuals to walk in their God given destiny. He is the author of Life in His Presence, The Returns to Bethel and Breaking Through into Harvest. He also leads prayer groups, mentors individuals and leaders and ministers to Pastors around the world.

As a successful entrepreneur, Michael established a private investment company and an engineering consulting company in Houston, Texas. As an accomplished Petroleum Engineer he is recognized as an industry expert in Hydraulic Fracturing. He has coauthored technical papers and provides expertise in production optimization to Oil and Gas companies. Michael and his wife Latasha have an adult son Ryan and two daughters, Anna and Abbey.